Dundee's Hampden Heroes

by

Kenny Ross

First published in Great Britain 2012

Text copyright Kenny Ross
Cover design by David Young

ISBN 978-0-9574353-0-8

Printed by Winter and Simpson Print, Dundee
Telephone 01382 813813

Contents

runners-up spot in the league.

In just five short years however, George Anderson had taken Dundee from Division Two also-rans to Championship contenders. Despite coming close to winning a haul of trophies, the facts showed that in the first fifty-six years of their existence only the Scottish Cup had been won by The Dee with five runners-up spots in League and Cup and six semi-finals appearances to their name.

A massive psychological block had to be overcome and some changes would have to be made by Anderson to turn the Dark Blues into winners and what he did next would not only transform Dundee Football Club but also shock the footballing world.

Foreword

WHEN I FIRST set my eyes on Dens Park, the grass was in the process of being cut. The groundsman was cutting the grass diagonally and it looked a picture. With the help of the shining sun, the whole picture was complete.

Mr. George Anderson had signed me and took me from my home in Aberdeen to Dundee to introduce me to my future 'work-place'. He saw the look on my face and asked my thoughts. I said I hadn't seen anything like it – it was just beautiful – if you could call a football field beautiful. The turf seemed to me like velvet and I wondered if I could ever reach the football standard that the field deserved. It was a challenge I had to face.

At that time Dundee F.C. had many fine players in their ranks and they were only too pleased to give their knowledge to an aspiring recruit like me, among others. Reg Smith became the coach after his playing days were over and Reuben Bennett became the fitness trainer, so the young players there were fortunate to be under their influence. Their knowledge was precious and I was only too pleased to take on board their valuable advice.

As the years rolled on, I found a host of players (too many to mention) that were fine members of Dundee F.C. They all carried the Dark Blue colours with distinction and I found it a pleasure and an honour to have played with them.

Winning the League Cups in consecutive seasons was a massive boost to the thousands of our fans who flocked to Hampden to witness football history being made and I was so happy to be a part of it all.

I just hope in future that any new players coming to play for the Club will give Dens Park and their fans the respect they both deserve.

Wishing the manager and the players all success in the future.

Yours Sportingly,

Doug Cowie

Best Wishes

Doug Cowie

Introduction

THE SEVEN YEARS after the Second World War is the most successful period in the distinguished history of Dundee Football Club. Having found themselves in the second tier when the League football resumed, the Dark Blues won back to back 'B' Division titles before they were granted promotion and followed that up with a runners-up spot in the 'A' Division two years later. In 1951 and 1952, Dundee won their first silverware since 1910 with two League Cup victories, becoming the first club to successfully retain it and sandwiched in between those victories was a Scottish Cup Final appearance, making it three major cup finals in a row. Add to that four Forfarshire Cups, three Dewar Shields and four Inter-City Cups, a total of fifteen trophies were won between 1945 and 1952. It was a golden era at Dens Park.

George Anderson transformed Dundee after he became manager in 1944 and turned them into a major force in Scottish Football. He got the reward for his 'think big' policy when Dundee defeated Rangers in the 1951 League Cup Final and history was made when that success was repeated against Kilmarnock twelve months later.

With the 1952 Scottish Cup Final also reached it meant the Dark Blues had appeared in three Hampden Finals in a row and a generation of Dundee fans had their first ever Hampden Heroes to worship. Never before had Dark Blues won a trophy at the National Stadium, with the club's only other success a Scottish Cup win over Clyde at Ibrox in 1910 and now they had done it twice in quick succession. It was a wonderful achievement.

It is however an achievement which is often forgotten or overshadowed by Dundee's Scottish League Championship win in 1962. As the League Cup triumphs share an anniversary with Dundee becoming Champions of Scotland ten years later, it is the League Flag win and the subsequent run to the European Cup semi-final which are regularly celebrated by the club. The League Cup wins are often an afterthought and this therefore is an attempt to redress the balance and tell the story of Dundee's Hampden Heroes from the early Fifties.

George Anderson built a wonderful side with some of the finest players to ever grace not only Dens Park but also Scottish Football. Amongst them was superstar Billy Steel for whom Dundee paid a world record fee, who could turn a game in an instant with his fantastic array of skill; there was the potent centre-forward Bobby Flavell, a football outcast who returned to Scotland to score in two League Cup Finals for The Dee; Bill Brown, the wonderfully agile keeper amongst the greatest custodians Scotland has ever produced and there was the famous half-back line of Tommy Gallacher, Doug Cowie and Alfie Boyd upon whom much of the success was built.

The local press nicknamed them the 'League of Nations' as Dundee led the way with bringing in players from different countries; most notably an elegant South African full back named Gordon Frew, his countryman Ken Ziesing who was a powerful centre forward before he was converted into a wing half at Dens and a left back, Jack Cowan, a rangy Canadian who became his continental player of the

year in 1951. Anderson made Dundee a power in the land by shrewd signings, a public relations touch ahead of his time and a fantastic team to boot who played some scintillating football.

This book tells the story of that team and to honour the players who played in the three Hampden finals, it has their biographies interspersed between the narratives. This therefore is their story – this is the story of Dundee's Hampden Heroes.

Acknowledgements

THE AUTHOR WOULD like to acknowledge the help, support and advice from Mark Robertson, Norrie Price, David Young, Tommy Young, Jim Gellatly, Ron Gellatly, Iain Munn, Alan Pattullo, Alasdair Leslie, Paul Wear, Chris Gavin of Aberdeen F.C. and Brian Chalmers and Alan Brown from printers Winter and Simpson. Special thanks has to go to Jim Davie for undertaking the difficult and arduous task of proof reading and editing and to Hampden Heroes Jimmy Toner and Doug Cowie. Doug Cowie in particular deserves thanks for his fantastic foreword and it was an honour to have the man who has made the most appearances in the club's history, has two League Cup winners' medals and is the only Dundee player to have played in two World Cups, write it.

The author would like to acknowledge the information in Norrie Price's *Up Wi' the Bonnets* and *They Wore the Dark Blue*, Jim Hendry's *Dundee Greats*, Jim Wilkie's *Across the Great Divide* and Bob MacAlindin's *Billy Steel: Scotland's Little Maestro*. These superb books have been an invaluable source of information alongside the newspapers of the day. The author acknowledges the use of illustrations and photographs from past and current newspapers, plus Dundee Football Club and, while every effort has been made to trace the ownership of illustrations, apologies are given should copyright inadvertently have been infringed.

There were 281,145 fans at the three Hampden Finals and my Dad, who is now sadly in the High Stand, was at each of them. Hearing about them as I grew up inspired me to write this book and made me dream of a day when I'll see Dundee win a cup at Hampden for myself. It is to these dreams and the dreams of Dundee fans everywhere that I dedicate this book as we continue to follow the rollercoaster of our wonderful club.

Chapter 1:
'Second Is Nowhere'

"WELCOME! THRICE WELCOME! to the year 1893, For it is the year that I intend to leave Dundee", wrote poet William McGonagall in his New Year's Resolution poem but if he did so, then he would have been unfortunate enough to miss the birth of Dundee Football Club who were founded that year and their first ever game which was played at West Craigie Park against Glasgow Rangers on August 12th.

Dundee F.C. were formed from the amalgamation of two local clubs, Our Boys and East End and their merger formed the basis of an application to join the three-year-old Scottish Football League into which they were admitted in June 1893.

Their first match took place therefore at the home of Our Boys with their colours being the sky blue and white strips of East End and on the 'Glorious Twelfth', Dundee's first match ended 3-3 with Sandy Gilligan having the honour of scoring the club's first goal.

By the end of their debut season, Dundee had moved to a new ground at the city docks at Carolina Port where a smoking slag heap on the adjacent gasworks on the Broughty Ferry Road side, nicknamed 'The Burning Mountain' often gave hundreds of fans a free view of the game.

In March 1894, goalkeeper Francis Barrett, centre-half William 'Plum' Longair and left winger Sandy Keillor became the first Dundee players to represent Scotland in a 2-1 victory over Ireland in Belfast and two years later Keillor became the first Dundee player to score for Scotland in a 4-0 triumph over Wales in the first and only international to be held at Carolina Port.

'The Port' had a superb playing surface but it was too remote, with no public transport links and, in 1899, Dundee moved to their current home. Dens Park was officially opened against St. Bernard's on August 19th 1899 when Fred McDiarmid was awarded a medal for scoring the first goal on the new ground and the move was the start of the good times for The Dee.

Twelve months previously, Dundee were saved from liquidation after poor gates had contributed to large debts and part of the new committee's strategy was to increase attendances by relocating to the new ground. It was a move that paid off, as the crowds started to flock to Dens and with Dundee now regularly playing in the dark blue of Our Boys, they finished as runners-up in the Scottish League championship three times within the next decade.

Silverware was also just around the corner and in 1910 Dundee won their first major honour when they brought home the Scottish Cup for the first time in the club's history. After a marathon ten-game campaign, Dundee won the oldest football trophy in the world after a 2-1 win over Clyde at Ibrox in the second replay. Jimmy Bellamy scored the equaliser after the Bully Wee had taken the lead and it was John 'Sailor' Hunter who wrote his name into Dundee folklore by scoring the winning goal.

It would be another forty-one years before Dundee would win another major honour, although they did reach the Scottish Cup Final again in 1925 where they lost 2-1 to Celtic who scored two late goals after Davie McLean had given Dundee a half-time lead.

Fourteen years later, when Scottish League football was suspended on September 3rd 1939 due to the outbreak of the Second World War, Dundee FC had plummeted to the lowest position in its forty-six year history (and were never to date to sink so low again). Despite sitting top of the Scottish League Division Two with maximum points after four games, the future did not look bright after the club had failed to win promotion the previous season, in what was their first ever outside the top division.

Dundee had been relegated for the first time at the end of season 1937/38 and had been expected to bounce back immediately. Despite reputedly having the richest directorate in Scottish Football in the guise of 'Jute Barons' Simpson, Graham, How and Galloway, they failed to make an impact and finished way off the promotion pace in sixth.

Gates at Dens had also hit an all time low with a paltry 1700 present to witness the last home game of the season against Dumbarton in April. By the time the new season arrived, Dark Blue pessimism was rampant but events at Dens were paling into insignificance compared to those on the world stage.

Just 2000 fans turned out at Broomfield to see Dundee defeat Airdrieonians on August 19th but when it was announced two days later that Hitler and Stalin had signed a non-aggression pact, it did not stop the Government preparing for war. Football was the last thing on people's minds and in Dundee children were evacuated in the main to the rural area of Kincardineshire while air-raid shelters were constructed and gas masks acquired.

Dundee did give their fans something to shout about on August 30th when they defeated Dundee United 6-1 at Dens in the Forfarshire Cup (Charlie McGillivray getting a hat-trick) but two days later, Hitler invaded Poland and Britain and France responded with a declaration of war.

Although the Scottish League suspended its competition immediately, it soon became clear that football would help sustain the morale of the nation and by October, new regional leagues were formed. Dundee entered into the new Eastern Division as crowds were limited to 8000 for fear of German air-raid attacks, but The Dee struggled to compete as players either volunteered for military service or were called up. With an average crowd of just 3000 and a £1400 financial loss for the season, Dundee decided in May 1940 to close for the duration of the conflict and Dens Park was used by the Decontamination (Food) Service until football resumed four years later.

The break however was vital for the restructuring and future of Dundee Football Club as, during this period, directors William Hood, Robert Paterson and James Meechan retired and vice-chairman David How died. The shares of Simpson and How were purchased by a local consortium and at the club's A.G.M. in April 1944, a new board was elected with consortium members John Thomson, James Gellatly, Murray Wilkie, Jack Swadel and – most significantly – George Anderson co-opted onto the board. With the tide of the war turning in the Allies' favour, preparations began in August 1944 for Dundee to resume playing football with George Anderson placed in charge of team affairs.

Anderson had been a director of his hometown club Aberdeen and had been put in charge of team affairs at Pittodrie when manager (and Dundee goalscoring legend) Davie Halliday went off to war. Anderson revelled in the position of caretaker-manager but as the job was being held open for the return of Halliday, Anderson made a move for the position at Dens. He had guested for Dundee during the First World War and now used his many contacts to build a new team and when Dundee returned to play in the Scottish League North East Division in October 1944, the team contained only two players who had played in the final game four years earlier.

On August 5th 1944, two months after the D-Day landings, Dundee returned to action against the British Army, in effect an almost entirely international eleven which included Matt Busby, Joe Mercer and Frank Swift. Despite The Dee going down 7-0, Busby complimented their *"cultured style of play"* and a week later, Dundee opened their league campaign in Kirkcaldy against Raith Rovers.

Dundee won the Scottish League North East Division First Series in 1944/45 and the Scottish League 'B' Division the season after but the club had to wait until it had won a third 'championship' in a row in 1946/47 before it was granted promotion. Due to the large number of guest players used by clubs and the number of players still being demobbed, the Scottish League decided not to re-insert promotion or relegation until 1947. After ten years out of the top flight, the Dark Blues were back in the big time for the start of the 1947/48 campaign and Anderson was the toast of the city.

Anderson, known affectionately as 'Toffee Dod' because of the confectionery business he ran in the Granite City, showed himself to be a forward planner and a progressive football thinker. He had constantly been gearing Dundee for life in the top flight and had been signing players with the 'A' Division in mind. Amongst those signings were future League Cup winning captain Alfie Boyd, club appearance record holder Doug Cowie and 2011 DFC Hall of Fame Inductee Tommy Gallacher, who had turned out for The Dee during the war.

Anderson also recruited English centre-forward Albert Juliussen who would write his name into the history books at Dens Park when, in consecutive games, he scored 'double' hat-tricks. On March 8th 1947, 'Big Julie' scored six goals at Alloa Athletic in a 10-0 win before bettering that in the next game a fortnight later with seven in a 10-0 victory at home to Dunfermline. Dundee would score a club record 113 goals on the way to winning their second 'B' Division title and those 10-0 wins still stand today as the club's highest ever victories.

Anderson was a master of man management and popular with the players with his emphasis on ball-work at training which was unusual at that time. He excelled in public relations and attempted to raise the profile of the club, but more importantly had an eye for talent and had constructed a skilful, attractive side in a relatively short space of time. So much so, that they were now ready for an assault on Scotland's elite.

Anderson still lived in Aberdeen where he was a town councillor and he travelled down to Dundee twice a week. The day-to-day training was left to assistants Willie Cameron and Andy McCall but the bowler-hatted, bow-tied, larger-than-life Anderson had the full support and respect of the players despite his infrequent appearances at the club.

It is said that Anderson would tell the players to 'go out and enjoy themselves' on a Saturday afternoon and he liked to encourage attractive football. Dundee's first season back in the top flight was rewarded with a fourth-placed finish in a sixteen-team league, their highest placing in twenty-six years and there were some memorable results along the way including a 4-1 home win over Celtic, a 6-0 win over Airdrie and a 7-0 win over Clyde. Perhaps the best result of all however was a 3-1 home win over Champions Hibernian on the last day of the season and it served notice that Dundee themselves were ready for an assault on the title.

In pre-season Anderson announced that none of his players were for sale and that young talent would be nurtured and the club practised exactly what Anderson preached. Of Dundee's thirty-two man squad for the 1948/49 season, twenty had been signed from juveniles or Juniors and several had been recruited from local clubs. Anderson had signed players from his home base in Aberdeen, including Doug Cowie, Syd Gerrie and young forward George Christie, whom he spotted playing for Banks O'Dee Juniors and to whom he gave a job in his Aberdeen sweet factory.

Things started well with only one defeat in the first nine and by mid-November Dundee lay second, just two points behind Hibs, and were through to the Scottish League Cup semi-final against Rangers.

The League Cup was still in its infancy with the idea emerging during the war when the S.F.A. suspended the Scottish Cup and the semi-final appearance was Dundee's best performance in the four years it had been running. The match against Rangers however, played in appalling conditions at

Hampden with a gale-force wind and torrential rain, was dogged with controversy as The Dee went down 4–1.

Rangers won the toss and opted to play with conditions in their favour in the first half so, having lost the choice of ends, Dundee should have been allowed to kick-off. The referee however insisted that Rangers kick-off and within a minute of the start, The Gers had taken the lead.

Dundee lost defender Tommy Gray, injured during the first goal, and within seven minutes were three down. Referee Livingstone would later receive a reprimand but it was little consolation for The Dee after losing 4–1 with Reggie Smith scoring a second half penalty.

Disappointment was short-lived however as by the time Rangers came to Dens on league business on January 3rd, Dundee lay one point behind the Ibrox team in second place. Dundee considered themselves unfortunate not to be level on points as Third Lanark's Polish winger Staroscik had fisted the ball into the Dundee net in the last minute to give the Hi-Hi's a draw three weeks earlier, but a win would now put Dundee top for the first time.

The official crowd of 39,375 was a new Dens Park record (and the sixth highest crowd ever on Sandeman Street) but it was estimated that there were another 6000 inside and another 5000 on the streets outside. Those who were lucky enough to see it witnessed a cracker as Marshall's early goal for Rangers was countered by an Ernie Ewen thunderbolt and a brace from Alec Stott to put The Dee into pole position.

Dundee stayed top for several months and also progressed to the Scottish Cup semi-final, where they faced Clyde, whom they had beaten to lift the trophy for the only time in 1910. After a 2–2 draw at Easter Road, Clyde won the replay 2–1 at Hampden, dashing Dark Blues hopes of a League and Cup double, but they were still favourites to win the Championship.

On the penultimate day of the season, Dundee defeated struggling Motherwell 2–1 at Dens in front of 26,000 fans and Rangers won 1–0 at Morton. Dundee had retained their one-point lead over the Ibrox side, which meant that a win in their final game at Falkirk would guarantee the League Flag, irrespective of Rangers' result at Albion Rovers.

On Saturday 30th April 1949, 17,000 crammed into Falkirk's sun-kissed Brockville Stadium but the thousands who had travelled from Dundee were blissfully unaware of the nerves flooding through their heroes in the dressing room. The normally effervescent and chirpy Anderson was unable to dispel them and, when confronted with the usual pre-match opposition banter, he locked his troops in the dressing room an hour before kick-off.

The tension built to such an intensity that by the time Dundee took to the field they looked thoroughly unnerved and gave the impression that they might freeze. It was an error of judgment by Anderson, who, in trying to protect his players from unnecessary distractions, now had to sit back helplessly as his team fell apart.

Mid-table Falkirk had little to play for and just before the interval Dundee were awarded a penalty when George 'Pud' Hill was brought down in the box after beating three men. Alec Stott, Scotland's leading goalscorer, had assumed spot-kick duties from Johnny Pattillo following the latter's miss at Love Street in an incredible 6–1 reverse in March. Stott's own record with penalties was flawless but he failed to make a clean contact with the ball and George Nicol in The Bairns' goal dived to his right to turn it round the post.

At half-time Dundee learned that Rangers were two up at Coatbridge and within eight minutes of the restart Dundee were two down to Falkirk. Stott pulled one back before Falkirk bagged another two goals and the final score of 4–1 was matched at Cliftonhill in Rangers' favour to allow them to claim the Scottish League Championship for the twenty-sixth time. They had also wrested their crown back after Hibs had usurped the title the previous season.

For Dundee, it was heartbreak. The season had ended with two cup semi-final defeats and a

Chapter 2:
Bill Brown

BILL BROWN WAS one of the greatest Scottish goalkeepers of the post-war period and is a legendary figure at both Dundee F.C. and Tottenham Hotspur. At Dundee he was a member of the 1951 League Cup winning side and represented Scotland in the 1958 World Cup. While at Spurs he was a member of the 1962 double winning side and part of the first British side to win a European trophy.

William Dallas Fyfe Brown was born in Arbroath on October 8th 1931 and played at outside-left as a youngster, only switching to goalkeeper when his Arbroath High School team's regular keeper had to go off injured and he was asked to go in goal. It was obvious from that day on that Bill was 'a natural' in goal and, but for that quirk of fate, Scotland may have been denied one of its greatest ever keepers as Bill had even had a trial for Scotland schoolboys as a winger.

After leaving school he began an apprenticeship as an electrician, whilst on the pitch he progressed from juvenile side Cliffburn to Junior club Carnoustie Panmure, before joining Dundee shortly before his 18th birthday. It was something of a coup for Dundee manager George Anderson to secure the services of Brown as he had been courted by various clubs including Manchester City, Sheffield Wednesday, Dundee United, Blackpool, Brechin City and hometown team Arbroath. Anderson, however, persuaded the seventeen-year-old to turn out for Dundee in a trial match against league champions Hibs to reopen Dundee Violet's Glenesk Park and playing against the Hibs 'Famous Five' forward line was enough to persuade the impressionable Brown to sign for The Dee.

Bill made his debut for the Dens Park club against Clyde at Shawfield in January 1950, but it took him several seasons to become the club's first choice keeper, sharing the goalkeeping duties for a few seasons with Johnny Lynch and Bobby Henderson.

Tall and slim, Bill was a safe, unflappable keeper who rarely needed to be spectacular. Quick and agile, he had good positional sense and great concentration, and playing behind Dundee's famous half back line of Gallagher, Cowie and Boyd he won his first honour when he was part of the Dundee side to win the League Cup in his third season.

Coming into the side in the final sectional tie against Raith Rovers when he saved a crucial penalty, Brown kept his place in the side for the two legged quarter-final against Falkirk and for the semi-final against holders Motherwell at Ibrox where The Dark Blues won 5-1 to book their place in the Final.

In front of 92, 325, Dundee clinched the trophy with a 3-2 win over Rangers and the side became instant local heroes, having brought the first major trophy back to 'Juteopolis' for forty-one years.

Bill missed both the 1952 Scottish and League Cup Finals due to being away on National Service but by 1954, he had made the yellow jersey his own. It wasn't just for Dundee however that he excelled as in 1956 he was honoured for his consistent performances with a Scotland 'B' cap against England. The following year he made three appearances for the Scottish League against the English

League, Irish League and the League of Ireland and as the World Cup in Sweden approached in 1958, Brown got two more League caps, again against the English League and the League of Ireland.

His performances for the Scottish League were impressive enough for the Scottish selectors to name him in the World Cup squad for Sweden and he got to make his full international debut in the tournament when he took over from Tommy Younger for the final group match against France.

Brown would go on to become the most capped custodian for Scotland with twenty-eight appearances, a record which stood until overtaken by Alan Rough in 1979. Of those caps he earned another three as a Dundee player when he played in all three matches of the 1959 British Home International Championships and it was in the game against England at Wembley in April that he caught the eye of Spurs manager Bill Nicholson who was in the process of strengthening his side.

Brown would make another three Scottish League appearances while at Dens Park before Nicholson put in an offer of £16,500 for him in June and the popular keeper was on his way to London after the Spurs boss took the night train to Dundee to secure the deal.

Characteristically calm and unfussy, yet breathtakingly acrobatic at need, Bill Brown was the last line of defence when Tottenham Hotspur became the first club in the twentieth century to lift the English League and FA Cup double in 1961, and two years later was a member of the team that thrashed Atletico Madrid 5-1 in the European Cup Winners' Cup Final, thus becoming the first British club to win a major European trophy.

Brown did not conform to the popular notion of what a goalkeeper should look like at the time for although he stood half an inch over six feet, his frame was sparse, stringy and seemingly insubstantial, in vivid contrast to the imposingly muscular individuals employed by most clubs to mind their nets. Every line of the Brown figure was angular, an impression emphasised by his aquiline features, although if some contemporary observers referred to him half-slightingly as willowy, there was no doubting his wiry resilience when it came to physical challenges with hulking centre-forwards.

Bill eventually left White Hart Lane in October 1966, spending a season with Northampton Town before emigrating to Canada where he played for Toronto Falcons. After retiring from the game he worked for a Toronto property developer and then spent many years in the employment of the Ontario Government Land Department and sadly passed away in Simcoe, Ontario at the end of November 2004 following a lengthy illness.

Brown's legacy at Dens was 274 appearances where he made sixty-two shut-outs, won one major trophy and gained thirteen Scottish caps at various levels and left a host of memories as a keeper who was elastically agile, endowed with remarkably sharp reflexes and was never less than impeccable for Dundee.

Honours at Dundee:	
Scottish League Cup winners:	1951/52
Scotland full caps:	4
Scotland B caps:	1
Scottish League caps:	8
Appearances:	
League:	215
Scottish Cup:	14
League Cup:	45
Total:	274

Chapter 3:
Record Breakers

GEORGE ANDERSON WAS beginning to transform Dundee into a cosmopolitan outfit, signing various Englishmen, two South Africans (Gordon Frew and Ken Ziesing), a Canadian (Jack Cowan) as well as several Scandinavians who came and went. He would later sign Scottish inside-forward Bobby Flavell fresh from playing in a non-F.I.F.A. sanctioned league in Colombia and a promising seventeen-year-old goalkeeper, Bill Brown, from Carnoustie Panmure and the Scots combined well with the imports, particularly the strong half-back line of Gallacher, Cowie and Boyd.

It was very much a transitional period and Anderson knew his master plan was far from complete.

With James Gellatly installed as chairman, Anderson had a largely free hand in transfer dealings and after the last day disappointment at Brockville, players came and went in an attempt to find a trophy-winning formula. Reuben Bennett, Jock Brown, Jack Bruce and George 'Piper' Mackay were released and Tommy Gray moved to Arbroath. Winger Johnny McIlhatton was signed from Everton for £5000 and full backs Alan Massie and Jack Cowan were brought in for free from Aberdeen and Vancouver University respectively.

There were additions also to the backroom team with recently retired Reggie Smith added to the staff as trainer-coach to join Jackie Kay (assistant manager), Willie Cameron (trainer-masseur) and wartime inside-left Andy McCall (reserve team trainer).

The 1949/50 season started with the League Cup sectional ties and in opening match against Clyde at Dens in front of 28,500 it needed a late equaliser by Ernie Ewen to earn a 1-1 draw. The next matches continued to disappoint and with confidence at rock bottom only three points were taken from sectional ties against Clyde, Motherwell and Partick Thistle as The Dark Blues finished last.

There had been a distinct lack of punch up front and Alec Stott had never really recovered from that last day penalty miss and failed to rediscover his lethal touch. He was replaced by recent signing from Aberdeen minor football Jimmy Fraser and by November a gradual recovery saw Dundee up alongside the Old Firm, just one point behind league leaders St Mirren.

It didn't last however as an eventual sixth placed finish was a disappointment and Anderson admitted that he was still a player or two away from a sustained challenge. Lynch, Pattillo and Ewen were reaching the veteran stage and so more players were brought in during the close season, including Arbroath centre-forward Ernie Copland, signed for £4000 after impressing in a Forfarshire Cup tie against Dundee.

Once again however, the Dark Blues struggled in the League Cup openers with only two wins from ties against Falkirk, St Mirren and Hibs. The game against Hibs at Dens had been abandoned after sixty-eight minutes due to flooding, with the visitors leading 2-0 but as the Easter Road side already had enough points to qualify out of the group, the match was not replayed.

The players were heavily barracked at Dens and although this was nothing new (and therefore not confined to the modern era), it had never been so widespread. Peter Rattray was a particular target and, upset by this treatment, he requested a transfer. Reluctantly, Anderson sold him to Plymouth in exchange for £7000-rated former Aberdeen forward Stan Williams, plus £3000.

Many fans were shocked by this move and in the next home game against Hearts, the 25,000 Dens crowd got right behind their team, helping to inspire them to a 1-0 win.

Willie Cameron decided to now retire and to replace him former Dens keeper Rueben Bennett became Reggie Smith's new assistant. Soon their newly devised training schedules had the Dundee players amongst the fittest in the land, with results starting to steadily improve, but Anderson still felt something was missing.

The genial managing-director was a highly persuasive character and although he had already signed stars like Juliussen, Gallacher, Cowie, Boyd and Brown amid fierce competition, none could compare with his next signing coup in September 1950, which confirmed just how far he had taken Dundee.

On September 21st Dundee FC called a press conference at Dens and a beaming Anderson entered the board room to declare, *"Gentleman, I want to introduce you to Billy Steel. Ex-Derby County and now of Dundee!"*

Dundee had paid The Rams £23,500 for the Scotland international and in the process broke the world record transfer fee that had stood for eighteen years (the longest unbroken time for this record) for Bernabe Ferreya's transfer between Argentinean sides Tigre and River Plate for £500 less. The press were astounded and it was one of the transfer coups of the 20th Century.

Steel was a footballing genius and a legend; the George Best, the Paul Gascoigne, the David Beckham of his time. He was a headline-maker, scandal-maker, a pin-up boy, but most of all he was a fabulous footballer who brought power, skill and imagination to the Dundee forward line. The fee paid for him was extraordinary for its time and it was not surpassed in Scottish terms for over a decade (though it was beaten in world terms just a month later when Welshman Trevor Ford went from Aston Villa to Sunderland for £30,000). For a provincial club like Dundee to land a player of Steel's calibre shocked the football world.

At twenty-six years old, Steel was already an established international and had starred in Great Britain's 6-1 win over the Rest of Europe in 1947 and scored for Scotland in their 3-1 victory over England at Wembley in 1949. Steel was desperate to move back to Scotland after three years at Derby but when Anderson had an initial offer of £18,000 rebuffed and Steel accepted training facilities at Ibrox, it looked like he was heading for Rangers.

Anderson however used his persuasive charm and on September 16th 1950 invited Steel to a private lunch before taking him to the Rangers v Dundee match on the Dark Blues' team bus. The press who spotted this asked Steel what was happening and he replied that he had no idea what the future held and that the opening of his shop in Glasgow in two months time would naturally take up a lot of his time.

Anderson's personal touch had made all the difference and when he upped his bid to world record proportions a few days later, he was able to call that press conference to show off the man he felt would be the final piece of his Dark Blue puzzle.

It was a huge gamble for Dundee, not just in financial terms but also because of Steel's personality. He was volatile, sharp as a tack and his team mates were as likely to be on the end of a verbal volley as the opposition. He was not lacking in confidence however and when asked what it was like to be the most expensive player in the world, he replied, *"Nothing to it. When I left Morton I needed a suitcase to carry my share."*

Fears that Steel might not make an impact at Dens were blown away on his debut on September 23rd when 34,000 turned up against Aberdeen at Dens – 10,000 more than had been expected.

The usual football specials buses from Albert Square to Dens were cut in half due to the transport employees' decision to ban overtime but it didn't hinder the appearance of a massive crowd at Dens. With admission prices ranging from one shilling and sixpence (7½p) to five shillings (25p), Steel had at a stroke chalked £4000 off his transfer fee and he delighted the huge crowd with a virtuoso display and the first goal in a 2-0 win.

The signing of Steel, unusually for a sports story, had made the front page of *The Courier* and their match report on his debut was headlined with *"Debut of Steel Really Something Special"* and excitement in the coming weeks reached almost fever pitch. The huge crowds kept coming with 37,400 turning up at Dens on December 30th to watch a 2-0 win over Rangers (when Dundee became the first side in Scotland to wear continental rubber boots to combat the frost), 35,000 on January 2nd to see a 2-1 win over Morton and then 38,000 on January 28th for a Dundee v Dundee United Scottish Cup first round tie, the biggest ever attendance at a Dundee derby.

A 2-2 draw with United meant a replay four days later and a new Tannadice record crowd of 20,000 saw Billy Steel score the only goal of the game to put Dundee through.

In the next round, Dundee drew St Johnstone in Perth and set the Muirton Park record attendance of 29,972 (still St Johnstone's record crowd today and three thousand more than watched Dundee become Scottish Champions eleven years later) and after a 3-1 win, a Dens Park record crowd of 40,920 (the fourth biggest crowd ever at Dens) turned up to watch the quarter-final against Raith Rovers.

By early March, Dundee lay just two points behind leaders Hibernian but after losing the Scottish Cup quarter-final 2-1 to Raith, defeats in consecutive weeks by East Fife and Airdrie put paid to title hopes for another year. Dundee eventually finished third, ten points behind the men from Easter Road in first and on the same points as Rangers in second, behind them only on goal average.

Since Billy Steel's arrival, Dundee had been transformed but were still very much the 'nearly men' with no tangible prizes in the trophy cabinet. Could that all be about to change however in Steel's first full season at the club?

Chapter 4:
Gerry Follon

GERRY FOLLON'S CAREER was temporarily halted before it really got underway when World War Two broke out in the year he was signed from Lochee Harp and, considering he went on to play 301 times for Dundee, it is remarkable to think how many times he could have played had Hitler not enforced a six-year hiatus.

Follon's time at Dens coincided with an incredibly successful post-war period and he would go on to collect four winners' medals and two runners-up medals while at Dens Park as well as a Scottish League cap.

In his inaugural season, Gerry played ten games for Dundee in the Scottish League Eastern Division as a right winger and continued on the wing after the end of hostilities but it wasn't until the 1946/47 season when he moved to right back that he became a regular in the side and made the number two jersey his own.

Originally a G.P.O. engineer, Gerry went on to University to attain an honours degree in teaching and despite many tempting offers from Dundee manager George Anderson, he remained part-time during his spell at Dens. The flamboyant Dundee boss wouldn't usually accommodate part-timers in his first team but such were Gerry's skills that he bent his own rules to play the Geography teacher.

Gerry was part of the side that won back-to-back Scottish League B Division Championships and in 1948/49 he made forty-two appearances as Dundee were pipped by one point to the Scottish League A Division Championship after a last day disaster at Falkirk.

Silverware was just around the corner however as he played no mean part in the consecutive League Cup wins in 1951 and 1952 as Dundee became the first side to successfully defend the trophy.

Gerry played in all nine matches on the 'Road to Hampden' in the autumn of 1951 and in the tenth and ultimately successful League Cup Final match, he was part of the side which beat Rangers 3-2 with a last minute goal in front of a estimated 30,000 Dundonians in the crowd.

He played in seven of the ten matches in the 1952/53 League Cup campaign and was one of seven players to pick up a second cup winning medal when Dundee defeated 'B' Division Kilmarnock 2-0 with two goals from Bobby Flavell.

In between these two successes, Follon suffered more Dark Blue heartache to add to the disappointment of 1949, when Dundee lost out to Motherwell in the 1952 Scottish Cup Final.

Dundee were at Hampden for the second time that season after bagging the League Cup in October but the Final against Motherwell in front of a staggering 136,990 couldn't see Dundee do a Cup double with the Steelmen defeating the favourites 4-0.

"We just did not play at all that day," said Follon to the Dundee match programme in 1999, *"But all credit to Motherwell who were worthy winners. It was a huge disappointment not to lift the Cup and was my biggest disappointment of my time at Dens along with that 4-1 defeat at Falkirk in 1949."*

The second League Cup in October more than made up for the Scottish Cup defeat and it was a remarkable feat for Dundee to reach three national cup finals in a row at Hampden which were played in front of over a quarter of a million fans.

Gerry also played in the match in which Dundee's record home attendance figure was set when 43,024 watched a Scottish Cup second round tie against Rangers but unfortunately for Gerry, he was at fault for the second goal as Rangers won 2-0.

In Gerry's eighteen years at Dens, he also picked up international honours when he played for the Scottish League against the Irish League in 1947, not long after Dundee had returned to the top tier.

On leaving Dundee, Gerry signed for St. Johnstone where he teamed up with former team mate Johnny Pattillo at Muirton Park and then finished his career with a two-year stint in the Highland League with Keith.

In the 1960s, he returned to Dens Park in a coaching capacity to look after Bob Shankly's reserve side with Jimmy Toner, a post he left only on attaining promotion to deputy rector at Lawside Academy in Dundee.

Honours at Dundee:	
Scottish League Cup winners:	1951/52, 1952/53
Scottish League Championship runner-ups:	1948/49
Scottish Cup runners-up:	1952
Scottish League B Division champions:	1945/46, 1946/47
Scottish League cap:	1
Appearances, Goals:	
League:	215, 4 goals
Scottish Cup:	25
League Cup:	58, 1 goal
Other:	3
Totals:	301, 5 goals

Chapter 5:
Festival of Britain 1951

THE FESTIVAL OF Britain was staged between May and September 1951 and was the brainchild of Labour deputy leader Herbert Morrison as a *"tonic for the nation"* which was still suffering from the effects of the Second World War. Described by a newsreel of the time as giving an *"inexplicable lift to the heart"*, it aimed to recreate the feeling of a trip to the seaside and to 'cheer up' post-war Britain as it continued to rebuild.

The main focus of the Festival was an exhibition at the South Bank in London while a former World War Two aircraft carrier, HMS Campania, took a travelling version of the exhibition to various ports around the country, including Dundee, where 51,422 visited the ship at the George V Wharf during its ten day stay.

One aspect of life not affected at the end of hostilities in 1945 was the attendance at football matches which were on the up and the government was keen for clubs to play exhibition matches during the Festival. Indeed Dundee's average crowd in the season just ended had been 23,500 with a peak of 40,920 for a Scottish Cup quarter-final tie with Raith Rovers in March and clubs were now encouraged to play against other sides from different parts of the United Kingdom.

Dundee were happy to get involved and just ten days after their final game of the season against Partick Thistle at Firhill (a 1-1 draw in front of 20,000), headed south to the north-west of England to play their first Festival match against Bolton Wanderers, Nat Lofthouse et al.

Dundee themselves were quite a draw, having paid a world record fee of £23,500 for Billy Steel earlier in a season where they finished third in the Scottish League Championship behind winners Hibernian and second placed Rangers on goal average. A healthy 10,000 crowd turned up to watch a 2-1 win for The Trotters with Dundee's goal coming from Bobby Flavell who scored his first goal for the club on his debut.

Flavell had controversially left Hearts in 1950 to join a club in a breakaway league in Colombia not sanctioned by F.I.F.A. When he returned to Scotland eighteen months later to sign for The Dark Blues, the Tynecastle club still held his registration and, after a long, drawn out wrangle, he would be unable to make his competitive debut until the first game of the following season.

It would be well worth the wait however as Flavell would become Dundee's top scorer in his first season and would soon write himself into Dens Park folklore by scoring in two League Cup Finals.

After the Bolton game, Dundee returned home to play their second exhibition game against Reading three days later but it was more disappointment for the Dark Blues when they went down 6-2 at Dens.

The Dee's third match took place on May 16th when Belfast Distillery travelled across the Irish Sea to Dens and this time the Dark Blues enjoyed a victory with a comfortable 4-1 win in front of 6,000 fans. Bobby Flavell was again on target for his first goal at home, while an Ernie Ewen brace and a goal from Ernie Copland completed the scoring.

Dundee United had also played an exhibition game away to Millwall on the same day as the

Reading game but fared no better with a 3-1 defeat but both city clubs were now 'encouraged' to face up against each other and agreed to complete the 1950/51 Forfarshire Cup Final which was still outstanding.

In front of 12,500 at Dens on May 19th, The Dee went down 3-2 to their neighbours with Ernie Ewen again on target alongside Tommy Gallacher and the game is listed amongst the official exhibition matches of the Festival of Britain.

As well as playing matches against other British sides, clubs were also encouraged to go on tour during this period to promote the U.K. and the national sport and to show teams abroad how to play the game 'we' invented. Since the war Dundee had undertaken tours to West Germany, Austria, Italy, Denmark, Sweden and Belgium and were only too happy to go on their travels in these pre-European club competition days.

This time the club decided to go on a one-month tour of Israel and Turkey and became the first side from the U.K. to tour Israel since it declared Independence from the British Mandate for Palestine in 1948. That declaration had led to the Arab-Israeli conflict but since the 1949 Armistice Agreement, the region had been deemed more stable and the British government were delighted that Dundee were to 'fly the flag' in their former protectorate.

A side touring from abroad was therefore a great novelty for the Israeli footballing fans and public and an impressive 50,000 turned up for Dundee's first match against Maccabi in Tel Aviv on May 30th. The tour got off to the best possible start when goals from Flavell and Copland gave The Dee a 2-0 win and a second victory was secured in Tel Aviv four days later against Hapoel, when a Doug Cowie penalty was the difference between the sides.

Dundee's third and final match in Israel was this time against a Maccabi-Hapoel Select on June 6th but they proved to be too strong for The Dee, running out 2-1 winners in front of 25,000 spectators.

Dundee now moved onto Turkey to play a further five matches and the first was a 2-2 draw with Genclerbirligi in the capital Ankara.

The remaining four matches were played in Istanbul, the first against an Istanbul Select and it proved to be a match of mixed emotions for Bobby Flavell. As the Dark Blues ran out winners by five goals to three, Flavell had grabbed a brace alongside two from Jimmy Andrews and one from Tommy Gallacher, but he was sent off when he retaliated against some rough treatment from a Turkish defender.

However, in the next match against Galatasaray, Flavell scored his first hat-trick for The Dee in a 6-0 win in which Ernie Copland also got a treble.

Galatasaray however got their revenge with a 2-1 win over Dundee on June 23rd and the final match of the tour finished in a 2-2 draw when Dundee again met an Istanbul select.

After a month away, Dundee returned home but their commitments to the Festival of Britain didn't end there as they were now due to take part in the St Mungo's Cup. The competition was the S.F.A.'s contribution to the Festival and was contested between fourteen Scottish 'A' Division clubs together with Clyde and Queen's Park from Division 'B'.

Celtic defeated Aberdeen 3-2 in the final after coming back from two goals behind in front of a crowd of 81,000 at Hampden Park but for Dundee, their interest ended in the first round when they lost 4-3 to Motherwell at home on July 15th. Two goals from Billy Steel and a third from 'Pud' Hill weren't enough to see Dundee through but after journeying by plane, train and boat to take part in eight games in three and a half weeks, it is no surprise that The Dark Blues crashed out at the first hurdle and the players could now enjoy a rest.

The new season started just three weeks after that Motherwell game but their punishing summer schedule didn't do Dundee any harm as they went on to reach the two major Cup Finals and win their first silverware in a generation.

Chapter 6:
Jack Cowan

JACK COWAN WAS a Canadian left back who played for Dundee F.C. from 1949 until 1954 and was a member of George Anderson's successful trophy-winning Dees in the early Fifties.

Born in Vancouver on June 6th 1927, Cowan became the first Canadian to play professional soccer in Europe when he signed for Dundee from the University of British Columbia in 1949. He also became the first Canadian to win a major football honour when he was part of the Dundee side which won the League Cup in 1951.

Cowan entered U.B.C. in Vancouver in 1945 to study electrical engineering and, as well as playing for the University soccer team, he also played for Pacific Coast League team Vancouver City between school terms.

At U.B.C., he was awarded with five Big Block Awards for excellence in varsity sports and in his first spell with Vancouver City he was awarded with the prestigious Rookie of the Year Award.

Upon finishing his degree, Cowan decided that there might be an opportunity to make a career out of playing soccer and to do so, he realised he would have to move to Europe to have a chance.

His opportunity came in 1949 when he was selected to play for the British Columbia All Star Team who were to travel to England to play two exhibition matches against Newcastle United and it was in these matches that he was spotted by ex-Dunfermline manager and ex-referee Bobby Calder, who was a friend of fellow Aberdonian, George Anderson. Calder recommended Cowan to the Dundee manager who then moved to bring him to Dens and he would turn out to be one of Anderson's most astute signings, making 149 appearances in the next five years.

Cowan joined Dundee at a time when things were just starting to tick. He made his Dark Blue debut in the first league match of the 1949/50 season away to Stirling Albion in a 2-2 draw and it was against 'The Binos' that Cowan scored his only goal for Dundee in a 4-1 home win on December 22nd 1951 in front of 17,000 fans.

His home debut came the following week against Queen of the South and in both matches he would wear the number three shirt that he wore in every single match he played for Dundee.

At the end of his first season, Cowan picked up his first winner's medal when Dundee beat Brechin City 3-2 in the final of the Forfarshire Cup but his greatest moment in a Dark Blue shirt came in an altogether bigger final eighteen months later.

On October 27th 1951, Dundee lined up to face Rangers in the Scottish League Cup Final and in a classic encounter Dundee edged out the Light Blues 3-2 with a last minute winner from skipper Alfie Boyd.

It was Dundee's first trophy in forty-one years and for Jack Cowan the first professional medal won by a Canadian player and both Cowan and Dundee very nearly made it two six months later in the Scottish Cup. In April 1952, Cowan lined up for Dundee against Motherwell at Hampden and although the Dark Blues were favourites, it wasn't to be as Motherwell scored four second half goals without reply to take the Scottish Cup back to Lanarkshire.

Before that Final however, Cowan was named as the North American Football Confederation (N.A.F.C.) Player of the Year for 1951 after his terrific displays for Dundee and his League Cup winning achievement. In 1961, the N.A.F.C merged with the Football Confederation of Central America and the Caribbean (C.C.C.F.) to form the Confederation of North, Central America and Caribbean Association Football (C.O.N.C.A.C.A.F.) and become the modern day governing body for football in the region. Cowan is now listed therefore as the C.O.N.C.A.C.A.F. Player of the Year for 1951 as the winners from both federations were absorbed into the list for the new Association. It was a tremendous accolade for Jack who became the first Dundee player to be awarded with any player of the year award outside of the club.

There was to be more final disappointment for Cowan however in October 1952 when he was unfit to play to in Dundee's third appointment at the National Stadium in twelve months, when they successfully defended their League Cup trophy against 'B' Division Kilmarnock.

Cowan had played in all nine matches on the 'Road to Hampden' and so was bitterly disappointed to get injured the week before the Final in a league match against Hearts at Dens. He was originally picked to play when the team was announced on the Thursday but after a fitness test on Friday, declared himself not fit enough to play, fearing letting his teammates down. He was replaced in the side by South African Gordon Frew but there was some consolation for Jack as he watched his side retain the trophy with a 2-0 win.

Whilst at Dens, Cowan was selected to play for both the Scottish International team and the Irish International team but he was unable to qualify because he was not of direct Scottish or Irish descent.

In his final season at Dens, Cowan made the decision to return to his native Canada but The Dee were unwilling to let one of their stalwarts go and made him a very good offer to stay. When he turned down the offer, Dundee tried to prevent him from continuing his football career, but an appeal to F.I.F.A. allowed him to sign for Vancouver Halecos and return 'home' with his Dundonian wife.

In his first season back at the Halecos (they had changed their name from Vancouver City who Jack had played for before joining Dundee), he captained them to the 1955 Dominion Soccer Championships and would go on to represent the Canadian national side.

He also played many games for the British Columbian All Stars and played for a Canadian All Star team against Lokomotiv Moscow in Toronto in 1956 but when selected to play for Canada away to Mexico in a World Cup qualifier later that year, he turned down the invitation and decided to retire from football at the age of twenty-nine to concentrate on his engineering career.

In 1974, Cowan was inducted into the British Columbia Sports Hall of Fame and in May 2000 he was honoured to be one of the first inductees in the Canadian Soccer Hall of Fame and was listed in their Canadian Team of the Century.

It is surely only a matter of time before a similar honour is bestowed upon him at Dens and he is inducted into the Dundee Hall of Fame.

Honours at Dundee:

Scottish League Cup winners:	1951/52
Scottish Cup runners-up:	1952
C.O.N.C.A.C.A.F. Player of the Year:	1951

Appearances, Goals:

League:	115, 1 goal
Scottish Cup:	13
League Cup:	21
Totals:	149, 1 goal

Chapter 7:
A Tournament Discovered

THE IDEA OF a League Cup came about almost as an accidental by-product of the Second World War, although James Bowie of Rangers had floated an astonishingly similar idea in an article in the *Sunday Mail* in May 1939. In season 1940/41 there were only sixteen clubs still playing league football in Scotland and these sixteen constituted the entire membership of the Southern League. By this time the Government wanted as much football played without undue interference with the war effort and as the S.F.A had suspended the Scottish Cup for the duration of the conflict and the Southern League programme only offered thirty matches as opposed to the thirty-eight in the pre-war Division One, there was a considerable gap in the football calendar.

In the spring of 1941 it was decided therefore to institute a League Cup competition with four sections of four teams who would play each other home and away on a league basis from an unseeded draw. One team from each section would qualify to produce two semi-finals which would be decided on a traditional knock-out basis.

Of the war-time competitions which were the responsibility of the Southern League and not the Scottish League, Rangers virtually monopolised the honours. From six competitions, they won four, lost a fifth by a corner to Hibernian (corners were used in the event of a draw in these pre-penalty shoot-out days) and that after losing their goalkeeper Jerry Dawson with a broken leg early in the match.

Their only other reverse was in the last Southern League Cup Final in 1945/46 when Aberdeen won 3-2, interestingly still officially called the Southern League Cup despite the illogicality of including Aberdeen in any such tournament. Aberdeen lists this victory on their official honours alongside the other Scottish League Cup victories in their history despite this being officially a different tournament with a different organisation. They did however reach the final of the first official Scottish League Cup the following season.

Rangers defeated them 4-0 in that 1946/47 final as part of what turned out to be a double revenge on The Dons by the men from Govan. After Aberdeen won the Southern League Cup, the trophy was taken back by the S.F.A for the competition known as the Victory Cup, a tournament organised to celebrate the end of the Second World War and presented it to Rangers a month later after they beat Hibs 3-1 in the final.

Dundee played in the Southern League Cup just once in 1945/46, a year after coming out of abeyance and in their first match defeated new club Stirling Albion 2-0 at Annfield in the first ever meeting of the clubs. Dundee were in a three-team section with Arbroath and The Binos and topped their group with five points from four games, but in the quarter-finals went down 3-1 to Rangers at Hampden.

The Southern League Cup had been such a success that when peace-time football resumed there was no thought of jettisoning it and the Scottish League introduced their own League Cup competition for the first official season of league football in 1946/47. Known therefore as the Scottish League Cup, a new trophy was gifted by the president of the Scottish Football League, Mr John McMahon, and was moved from the end of the season to start in early September before being won by Rangers in April in front of 82,700.

The competition would start on a sectional basis with clubs being put into groups from sides of the same division meaning that there were either sections of 'A' Division teams or 'B' Division teams. With the section winners going through to the quarter-finals, the lower league sides stood a great chance of getting through to the last eight and facing one of the 'big boys.'

Dundee were drawn in Section F in a three-team group alongside Stenhousemuir and Raith Rovers and in their first ever League Cup tie defeated Raith 2-0 in Kirkcaldy with two goals from Johnny Pattillo. The first ever League Cup match at Dens saw a 4-0 victory for The Dark Blues over Stenhousemuir with Ernie Ewen getting a hat-trick and Dundee topped their section with a 100% record.

The quarter-final draw was seeded with 'A' Division sides guaranteed to play 'B' Division sides and Dundee were pulled out of the hat alongside Aberdeen. In the first leg at Dens, the Dark Blues were unlucky to go down 1-0 in front of 28,300 fans and they couldn't overcome the deficit in the second leg, despite two goals from Albert Juliussen as they went down 3-2 at Pittodrie, to go out 4-2 on aggregate.

The League Cup got off to a great start because it had been instituted at a time when the post-war football boom was coming to a height. Moreover, no club monopolised it in the first fifteen years after the war with seven different winners. East Fife won it three times – once as a Second Division club to add to their astonishing feat of winning the Scottish Cup in 1938 while in the same division – Hearts were likewise successful on three occasions, Dundee twice as the first club to retain it, Celtic twice and once each for Motherwell and Aberdeen. In this period Rangers, who before liquidation had the most wins with twenty-seven, only won it three times; far below their accustomed strike rate in future years.

Dundee's best performance in the first five years of the League Cup was the controversial semi-final defeat to Rangers in 1948 but success was just around the corner, unprecedented in the history of the club or the competition.

Chapter 8:
Tommy Gallacher

WHEN TOMMY GALLACHER signed full-time for Dundee in 1947, it had an impact on football in the City of Discovery that went way beyond the normal span of a player's career. To begin with he became part of the famous, trophy winning half-back line of Gallacher, Cowie and Boyd and then when he retired prematurely, he became Dundee's foremost football correspondent for local newspaper *The Courier and Advertiser* for whom he wrote for twenty-nine years.

Born in Renfrewshire as one of five sons of Scottish football legend, Celtic's 'Mighty Atom' Patsy Gallacher, it would perhaps seem only natural that he would follow in his father's footsteps and it was to Dundee's fortune that the cultured and classy wing half would spend eleven years at Dens Park.

To begin with, his father Patsy was keen that his son would take up the game on a strictly amateur basis and in 1942, with a number of clubs after Tommy, he signed for amateur side Queen's Park while working in his reserved occupation job in the labs at the Royal Ordnance establishment in Bishopton.

Towards the end of the war however, Tommy was keen to try something else and within weeks of leaving the labs, his call up papers were through his letterbox and he joined the Highland Light Infantry in January 1945. Stationed at the Bridge of Don barracks in Aberdeen, Gallacher worked as a P.E. instructor with the Army and was commanded by Colonel Jock McGregor, who was a friend of Dundee's Granite City born manager, George Anderson.

As was the norm during both wars, players turned out as guests for clubs near where they were stationed and towards the end of the season, Tommy found himself turning out for Aberdeen. At the start of the 1945/46 season however, Anderson used his influence with his friend to have Gallacher turn out sixteen times for The Dee as they won the Scottish League 'B' Division championship.

Dundee were denied promotion to the top tier due to the Scottish League declaring the season unofficial with so many players still in the armed forces and by the time Tommy signed full-time on his first professional contract in the summer of 1947, Dundee had won the 'B' Division for a second time so that Tommy's return to Dens coincided with the club's return to the top flight.

Tommy started his first full season with Dundee as an inside-right but soon he was to stamp his class and quality at Dens Park by wearing the number four jersey at right-half due to the intervention of his old army commander, Colonel McGregor. When wing-half Reggie Smith was set to miss a match at Parkhead due to a boil on his leg, Anderson was unsure who to replace the English international with and when he spoke to old buddy McGregor, he suggested to Anderson that he should play Gallacher at wing-half, having seen him play there for the army.

Despite this being a bluff, Gallacher very soon settled into his new position and the rest, as they say, is history as he struck up a partnership with Doug Cowie and Alfie Boyd to become part of perhaps the finest half-back line in Dundee's history.

In his second full season, Dundee really clicked into gear with Tommy playing in all forty-four league and cup matches as the Dark Blues finished runners-up in the Scottish 'A' Division Championship. Needing just a point on the last day at Brockville to win the title, Dundee lost 4-1 to Falkirk and gifted Rangers the League flag by a solitary point.

"We hit them with everything that day but we couldn't get the ball past their brilliant little goalkeeper, George Nicol," Tommy told author Jim Hendry in his superb *Dundee Greats* book. *"He was invincible that day and he even saved Alec Stott's penalty. It was a sad end to a tremendous season....... and in my opinion we were a far better side than the one a couple of years later when Billy Steel came."*

However, silverware didn't elude Dundee for long and that side with Billy Steel lifted the Scottish League Cup in October 1951. In front of 92,000 at Hampden, Dundee defeated Rangers 3-2 with goals from Flavell, Pattillo and Boyd but missed out on a cup double that season when they lost to Motherwell in the Scottish Cup Final.

Dundee did however achieve a cup double the following season after defeating Kilmarnock 2-0 in the League Cup Final but Gallacher missed the game after being dropped. He had previously fallen out of favour with George Anderson and was in and out of the side. Despite playing the week before the final against Hearts he was dropped from the side for the big day and lined up for the reserves at Dens.

Tommy continued to play for Dundee until 1956 but the beginning of the end came for Gallacher when Willie Thornton took over from Anderson in the Dens Park hot seat. Thornton wanted Tommy to play in his old position of inside forward but it didn't work out and he was keen to move on to pastures new. Falkirk and Dunfermline were interested but Dundee wanted a fee and wouldn't release him and at thirty-four he decided to hang up his boots and pursue a career with local publishers D.C. Thomson for whom he had been writing a column in their *Courier* newspaper for the previous eighteen months.

Football's loss was journalism's gain as he would write about football in Dundee over the next three decades, reporting on all of Dundee's major triumphs and European trips in the sixties and seventies.

It is however as a strong, forceful and creative wing-half that Tommy will be best remembered at Dens and it is a tragedy that he won only one Scottish League cap against the English League in 1949, often overlooked for the full side despite being in reserve eleven times. Tommy was inducted into Dundee's Hall of Fame in 2011 and with his deft touch, was a key figure in a team built on foundations of quality and finesse that brought glory in a golden age that is rightly revered in the club's history.

Honours at Dundee:	
Scottish League Cup winners:	1951/52
Scottish League Championship runners-up:	1948/49
Scottish Cup runners-up:	1952
Scottish League B Division winners:	1945/46
Scottish League cap:	1
Dundee F.C. Hall of Fame:	2011 Legends Award

Appearances, Goals:	
League:	200, 9 goals
Scottish Cup:	24
League Cup:	50, 2 goals
Other:	5, 1 goal
Totals:	279, 12 goals

Chapter 9:
The Road Begins

IN THE SUMMER of 1951, there was plenty of speculation in the press about the Dark Blues' prospects and one local paper, *The People's Journal*, described Dundee as a side *"with potential to win the Scottish Cup."* In many ways cup football was far more important to football fans during this period than the league championship as it provided a greater sense of occasion. At a time when few fans followed their team away, going 'Up for the Cup' still exerted a powerful hold and a potential trip to Hampden held a special appeal.

This was only logical as the Cup for many clubs was the 'holy grail'. The prospect of winning the Championship was remote for most while fewer teams got relegated and the financial repercussions were far less severe. There were no European places to play for and no pressure to finish in the 'top six' meaning that for a lot of clubs there was nothing to play for from one month to the next – except in cup competition. In fact, George Anderson was ahead of his time somewhat, regularly calling for a smaller league where matches would be more meaningful.

After five years, the League Cup was now fully entrenched in the Scottish football calendar and proving just as popular as the Scottish Cup in many respects with crowds for League Cup ties higher than for league matches between the same opposition.

The League Cup had, since 1949, become the traditional seasonal openers with sectional matches against sides from the same division and for 1951/52, Dundee were drawn against fellow 'A' Division sides Hearts, St. Mirren and Raith Rovers for the start of their 'Road to Hampden'.

With the end of season tour to Israel and Turkey and the St Mungo's Cup tie with Motherwell in July, Dundee didn't play any matches pre-season. The first chance the fans got to see their heroes in action was in the public trial on Monday 6th August which traditionally saw both the first team and the reserves play in mixed teams, 'the Blues' and 'the Whites'. A crowd of 5,500 turned up to see Anderson experiment with a new forward line of Flavell, Zeising, Toner, Andrews and Steel and *The Courier* reported that in particular *"the Flavell-Toner wing fitted together well and produced some of the best moments of the game."*

For Steel it was a return to Dens after he had played in Scotland's European summer tour but it had not been a happy trip for the mercurial inside-left. Steel had been a Scotland regular since his Morton days and two months after signing for Dundee, scored four for the national side in a 6-1 win over Northern Ireland in the British International Championship. He had started the tour well as the key man in a 5-0 win over Belgium in the Heysel Stadium but in the next match against Austria, he retaliated under severe provocation to become the first Scotland player to be sent off as they lost 4-0.

Much was expected of Dundee's star man for the coming season and he took his place at number 10 for the first game of the season away to St. Mirren in the Scottish League Cup, 'A' Division – Section C.

The forward line that had impressed in the trial game five days previously was retained but there were changes in the defensive set-up for The Dark Blues. Making his debut was goalkeeper Bobby Henderson who was signed on a free-transfer from Partick Thistle in May, taking over in goal from youngster Bill Brown who had finished the previous campaign between the sticks. He was brought to the club after veteran goalkeeper Johnny Lynch settled a dispute with the club and was freed after sixteen years at Dens and Henderson was chosen to start the season as number one.

Also coming into the side was South African Gordon Frew at left back who replaced Canadian Jack Cowan after he injured an ankle in training, but Frew himself got injured early in the match, receiving a bad thigh knock in a collision with The Buddies' Burrell.

It was part of a bad half for The Dee who only went over the halfway line three times in the opening forty-five minutes and with St. Mirren pressing high up the pitch, it was a surprise that they didn't go into the interval ahead.

"We might have been leading by four at half-time," said Saints manager Bobby Rankin post-match but the goalless half meant it was very much anyone's game.

The match was Bobby Flavell's competitive debut for Dundee after his transfer wranglings were finally sorted out and, after impressing on the tour to Israel and Turkey in May, he appeared to add the necessary punch to the forward line that had often been lacking the year before.

Season 1950/51 saw half-back Alfie Boyd finish as top goal scorer with a paltry eight strikes, four of which were penalties, but Flavell brought a predatory instinct that saw him score on his debut to put Dundee 2-0 up. Jimmy Toner had given Dundee the lead, scoring the Dark Blues' first goal of the season but the most impressive aspect of the performance was the interchanging positions with Ken Zeising which often kept St. Mirren guessing.

The Saints scored two late goals to earn a 2-2 draw but the result was considered *"a decent start"* by *The Sunday Post*. George Anderson declared himself *"satisfied"* with the point despite throwing away a two-goal lead, pointing to the fact that they effectively played the majority of the match with ten men after Frew's injury and had survived The Buddies' opening onslaught.

Hearts beat Raith Rovers 1-0 in the section's other match at Tynecastle and the Edinburgh side then had to travel to Tayside four days later to 'first-foot' the new season at Dens. With Frew out injured, Cowan was back in after making a recovery and the first home game of the season was much anticipated with *The Courier* claiming that *"a game against Dundee and Hearts usually means a feast of football."*

And boy, were they right with an absolute thriller for the 22,500 crowd from start to finish! Right from the first minute, Dundee keeper Bobby Henderson was forced to take the ball off Wardhaugh's toes before the Dark Blues went straight up the park and forced a corner when Toner's shot was turned round the post by Hearts' keeper Jimmy Brown. Minutes later Ken Zeising got the ball awkwardly from Toner near the goal line only to watch his effort roll agonisingly over the bye-line and then Alfie Boyd was knocked out stopping a full blooded Jambos' drive.

For the first half an hour it was anybody's game but the vital breakthrough came on thirty-one minutes for the Dark Blues. A sweet passing movement between Flavell and Toner ended with the former Junior laying the ball out to the right to Zeising and although it was an awkward angle, the South African sent an unbelievable shot past Brown to give Dundee the lead.

Shortly after the restart, Zeising sent a shot screaming over the bar but on forty-one minutes he wasn't to be denied when, after being played through by Toner, he hit the ball on the run to give Dundee a two-goal half-time lead.

Seven minutes into the second half, Hearts pulled one back when Wardhaugh headed in a Whitehead cross and for the next half an hour the Tynecastle side were well on top. The Dundee defence had to pull out all the stops to prevent an equaliser with Doug Cowie having what *The Courier*

described the next morning as *"one of his finest games at centre-half."*

Alfie Boyd was in the wars again when he got a slight cut over his eye going for a high ball, while Billy Steel was frequently back giving the defence a hand. The match continued to be a thriller right until the final minute when Gerry Follon kicked the ball off the line but The Dark Blues held on for a vital win to send them to the top of their section.

In the other match, Raith Rovers beat St. Mirren 3-2 at Stark's Park and while the Paisley side came back from two down in the previous match with Dundee, it was their turn to squander a two-goal lead as the Kirkcaldy side fought back to snatch victory in the second half.

That win however proved costly for Raith in injury terms as they struggled to put a side out at Dens three days later. Their main concern was goalkeeper George Johnson who was injured midweek and their injury woes continued in the first half when right-back Malcolm McLure had to be taken off with a shoulder injury.

Dundee took full advantage and ran out 5-0 winners with goals from Billy Steel, a hat-trick from Jimmy Toner and an own goal from Harry Colville. Raith's midweek matchwinner, centre-forward Penman, was played out of the game by Cowie while Gallacher and Boyd forced the play well. Toner's trio, which were all set up by Zeising, was his first treble for The Dee.

It was an important win for Dundee with five points from six in their opening three games and almost as important was the fact that Dundee's goal average also had quite a boost. In addition to the 'goals for' column, the other sides in the section had all conceded five after St. Mirren and Hearts drew 5-5 at Love Street and *The Sporting Post* pointed out that *'these fifteen goals might come in handy to the Dark Blues when qualifying time comes around'*.

Dundee's Saturday evening sports paper also quoted Raith manager Bert Herdman as saying, *"that was the worst game we've played in three years"* and claimed that Billy Steel had *"turned in one of his best performances in a dark blue jersey."* The Dee had given themselves a great chance of topping their section.

However, if there is one thing that Dundee have consistently done over their entire history, it's doing things the hard way and, after giving themselves a two point lead at the top, went on to lose their next two games.

The next match was seven days later on Saturday 25th August at home to St. Mirren but the night before that, Dundee 'A' took on Dundee United 'A' in a 'C' Division 'wee derby' at Tannadice. With George Hill, Johnny Patillo and George Christie in the side they drew 3-3 in front of 5,000 fans, with Christie getting a hat-trick.

For the Saints game, Tommy Gallacher had been a doubt after being in bed on Friday with a cold and a sore throat but he made the game while Gordon Frew played his second game in a row at left-back for the injured Cowan. Doug Cowie missed out after he kicked the ground in training and injured his toe which gave recent signing Bob Henderson the chance to come in for his debut. He was signed earlier in the week from Falkirk for £3000 but the centre-half had a shaky start as The Dee went down 1-0 thanks to a late goal from Gerry Burrell.

It had been a poor display from the Dark Blues which saw the Dundee fans starting a slow handclap in the second half. After the match, George Anderson had to deny to the press that the capture of Henderson from The Bairns would signal the departure of Doug Cowie in exchange for Bolton's Scotland international forward Billy Moir who had been a guest of the Dens Parkers in 1945.

The result, coupled with Raith's 2-0 home win over Hearts opened up the section so that any of the four teams could qualify. For Dundee to go through it was going to have to be a big effort with two away games in the last two matches and the first of those was away to Hearts at Tynecastle four days later.

In his first full training session with Dundee, Bob Henderson fell and was likely to be out for at least two weeks with a twisted his knee, but the good news pre-match was that Cowie was fit again to retake his number five shirt.

After his hat-trick in the 'wee derby' George Christie came in for Jimmy Andrews on the left wing and it all started so well for Dundee when Jimmy Toner sensationally scored in the first minute with a shot to the far corner after Zeising had headed a Flavell cross to him.

However, minutes later, Bobby Flavell picked up a knock and started to limp badly before Billy Steel also picked up an injury and by the sixth minute The Dark Blues found themselves 2-1 down.

Playing effectively with nine men, with Flavell and Steel stuck out on the wing out of the way in these pre-substitute days, Dundee were struggling and in twenty-three minutes found themselves 3-1 down when Bobby Parker scored his first penalty of the match.

Zeising pulled one back to make it 3-2 before Bobby Henderson in the Dundee goal 'rugby tackled' Hearts winger Urquhart nine minutes before half time and Parker hit home his second spot kick of the game to make it 4-2.

Hearts made it five on the stroke of half-time with the goal of the game when Cumming shot high into the corner of the Dundee net from eighteen yards to give the Edinburgh side a stunning 5-2 lead.

The pace slackened off in the second half but Dundee, playing in white, rarely threatened the Hearts defence with Flavell and Steel limping about on the left touchline. With no more scoring the match finished 5-2 which was enough to take Hearts off the bottom of the section and for Dundee to slip into second after St. Mirren beat Raith 2-0 at Love Street.

Just two points separated the four teams going into the last games and reporter Colin Glen in *The Courier* said that it was going to be *"a bonnie fecht"* to see who qualified. Dundee were one point behind leaders St. Mirren and a point ahead of Raith while Hearts were on the same five points as Dundee and the Tynecastle side fancied their chances of going through with a home tie against The Buddies whilst Dundee were at Raith who had won their previous two home games.

The 5-2 defeat in Edinburgh meant that there would be changes for the final group game; some enforced, some not. Dundee would have to line up without Billy Steel after he was ordered to completely rest for three or four days after Tynecastle and would be out for three or four weeks, meaning that the Dark Blues would have to start their league campaign without him.

Also doubts were Flavell, Zeising, Cowan and Andrews and, with so many injuries, Anderson decided that he would take the unusual step of not picking the team until lunchtime on Saturday. Dundee could only muster a travelling party of thirteen which included two goalkeepers and Ernie Ewen for the first time that season.

In the end Gallacher and Flavell missed out alongside Steel, who watched the game from the stand while Anderson decided to replace Bobby Henderson in goal with Bill Brown after Henderson had made some unforced errors against Hearts. Ewen, Irvine and Williams came in for the injured trio while Bill Brown quickly justified his inclusion with a penalty save from the unlucky Harry Colville who had scored an own goal in the first meeting.

Raith themselves had injury worries with four key players out and a Rovers' director said pre-match that the side Dundee would be able to field despite the injuries they had showed that they were *"stronger in reserve than any other team in Scotland including Hibs, Hearts and Rangers."*

He was proved right as the men who played a big part in earning Dundee's 3-1 win were the players who were brought in. Not only did Brown save a penalty at 0-0 but the goals came from George Christie (2) and Stan Williams and Brown put in a determined display after he had to have his fingers strapped at half time, injuring them turning the penalty round the post.

There was little between the sides over the ninety minutes but the missed penalty had dented

Raith's confidence and at full time Dundee were desperate to find out if the victory was enough to put them through. When the news came through that Hearts had beaten St. Mirren 3-1, calculations were needed with both Dundee and Hearts finishing top of the group on seven points and goal average required to split the pair.

Goal average was a system used before the advent of goal difference in 1970 and was calculated by dividing the number of goals scored by the number of goals conceded and in the end Dundee had a better average of 1.40 compared to Hearts' 1.25 to send The Dark Blues through.

The 5-0 home win over Raith had indeed proved crucial as The *Sporting Post* had predicted and the final Section C table was as follows:

Team	Pld	W	D	L	GF	GA	GAv	Pts
Dundee	6	3	1	2	14	10	1.40	7
Heart of Midlothian	6	3	1	2	15	12	1.25	7
St. Mirren	6	2	2	2	13	13	1.00	6
Raith Rovers	6	2	0	4	6	13	0.46	4

The oldest woman in Britain that day celebrated her 107th birthday, claiming she hated potatoes, tea and the wireless and Dundee celebrated also as not only were they through to the League Cup quarter-finals, but their 'A' team went top of the 'C' Division with a 5-1 win over Raith at Dens, again backing up the Rovers' director's claim of Dundee's strength in depth.

As the Dundee team bus drew up at Kirkcaldy Station to catch the train home, a crowd of a thousand Dark Blue fans gave them a huge cheer. They cared not a jot that their team had got out of their section by the finest of margins and when George Anderson said to the press, *"Getting out of the section was the key so don't be surprised by what we do next,"* they looked forward to Monday's draw with relish.

Chapter 10:
Doug Cowie

THERE ARE THOSE who would argue that Doug Cowie is the greatest Dee of all time and they certainly have a case. Cowie is the player with the most appearances in a Dundee shirt, is the only Dundee player to have played in two World Cups, won two League Cup winners' medals, was runner-up in the League Championship and Scottish Cup, won twenty full caps for Scotland, five League caps and one B international cap and is the club's longest serving player. His sixteen seasons in Dark Blue were to prove to be among the most successful periods in the club's history and he played alongside some of the greatest names Dundee has ever witnessed.

Cowie arrived at Dens in 1945 when the men of Dundee were returning from war with a craving for some return to normality centred on sport and the masses were returning to Dens Park in search of inspiration and solace to ease their hurt. Perhaps a form of escapism, they found new Dundee manager George Anderson was in the process of building a great team and he looked towards an apprentice riveter working in the John Lewis shipyard in Aberdeen to be one of his heroes.

Cowie was within hours of signing for his local side Aberdeen but Anderson was prepared to get his man and after a quick discussion with Doug's father who was working across the road, the young centre-half signed for Dundee from his Junior club Aberdeen St. Clements.

Doug played 446 competitive games for Dundee, a club record, but incredibly it could have been so much more. At the age of nineteen, he made his competitive debut on 23rd February 1946 in Dundee's first ever League Cup match at Stirling Albion, but it was his only appearance of the season. In the following year Doug played just three times despite featuring prominently in a pre-season tour of West Germany, Austria and Italy and one wonders just how many appearances he could have chalked up!

The highlight of his career came when Dundee won back to back League Cups against Rangers in 1951 and Kilmarnock in 1952 but he missed out on a treble when Dundee lost the 1952 Scottish Cup Final which was sandwiched between the League Cup triumphs. Doug was also part of the Dundee side which finished runners-up in the 1948/49 Scottish League Championship after they lost on the final day at Falkirk to hand the title to Rangers by one point.

He started his career at centre-half but always preferred to play left-half and became part of the famous half-back line of Tommy Gallagher, Doug Cowie and Alfie Boyd. Playing in either position made no difference to Doug as his skill and elegance were always on show and many Dundee players of the Forties and Fifties often quoted Doug as the best player they played alongside.

Amongst those was the legendary Billy Steel who signed for Dundee in September 1950 and who was known for putting his team mates on the sharp end of his tongue, but for Cowie he reserved his greatest compliment by stating that the Aberdonian could *"play a wee bit."*

In 1953 Doug made his international debut alongside Steel against England at Wembley and the 2-2 draw was the first of twenty caps which make him the second most capped player in the club's history.

In 1954 Doug became the first Dundee player to play at a World Cup when he played in two games in the Swiss finals against Austria (0-1) and Uruguay (0-7) and four years later in Sweden played in another two matches against Yugoslavia (1-1) and Paraguay (2-3) which turned out to be his last game for Scotland.

Cowie played under three managers at Dens, namely George Anderson, Willie Thornton and Bob Shankly and all three made Doug captain at one time or another.

However, on the eve of Dundee's greatest triumph, in the summer of 1961, Shankly decided to free the thirty-four year old Cowie, citing age as the reason why, but just a few weeks later, Doug was disappointed to see Shankly sign Gordon Smith, who was three years his senior. When Dundee went on to lift the League flag just twelve months later, it meant that Cowie was denied a league winners medal for a second time and despite that great triumph at Muirton, there were many who thought that Doug had been released just a little too early.

Near the end of his playing days in 1961 Doug still lived in a Dundee tenement which is changed days indeed from now. It should therefore be remembered that football then was a working man's sport and they were a different breed of player in those days. No agents, no fancy hair styles, no perms or after shave, no fancy cars or lucrative wages. Some came from the shipyards or coal mines to play for their professional sides and Doug Cowie was one of those gems. He was amongst a generation who played with a pride in their team that would put most modern players to shame when the elements rarely caused a match to be cancelled or anything other than a serious injury caused them to miss a game. They played with boots that covered their ankles, kicking and heading a ball that grew heavy if it rained, with a lace that hurt the head if by chance it met the napper straight on.

Always a gentleman, Doug was honoured by the Club when they named one of their·original hospitality lounges at Dens as the Doug Cowie Lounge. In his book *Dundee Greats*, author Jim Hendry described Cowie as a player with *'the touch of an angel'* and this angel was deservedly inducted into the inaugural Dundee F.C. Hall of Fame with a legends award in 2009. There is no doubt he deserves his place amongst the first of the elite to be honoured by Dundee in this way.

Honours at Dundee:

Scottish League Cup winners:	1951/52, 1952/53
Scottish League Championship runners-up:	1948/49
Scottish Cup runners-up:	1952
Scottish League B Division champions:	1946/47
Scotland full caps:	20
Scotland B caps:	1
Scottish League caps:	3
Dundee F.C. Hall of Fame:	2009 Legends Award

Appearances, Goals:

League:	341, 19 goals
Scottish Cup:	32, 1 goal
League Cup:	73, 4 goal
Totals:	446, 24 goals

Chapter 11:
"Don't Be Surprised"

THE DRAW FOR the League Cup quarter-final took place at the Scottish League headquarters in West Regent Street in Glasgow on Monday 3rd August and for the first time in the competition's history the draw was going to be an 'all-in' unseeded draw. The other seven teams in the draw alongside Dundee were Rangers, Celtic and Motherwell from the 'A' Division and Dunfermline, Falkirk, St Johnstone and Forfar from the 'B' Division and in the event the 'A' Division clubs all drew a side from the lower league.

The Courier described it as a *'freak of the ballot box'* and 'this freak' threw the Dark Blues together with Falkirk. While pulling a 'B' Division side out of the hat might have been seen as a favourable draw, George Anderson knew it was anything but and would not be easy. By the time of the first leg on September 15th, Falkirk were the only unbeaten side in the top two divisions, had a 100% record in their League Cup section, which included two victories over Dundee United (3-0 at Brockville and 1-0 at Tannadice), had scored twenty-three goals in their six ties, conceding just four, and had Scotland's leading scorer in their ranks, Angus Plumb, who had thirteen goals to his name already.

Added to that, the Dark Blues had no love for Brockville after their last day disaster two years before which it was still very fresh in the memory for the majority of the squad and for Anderson himself.

It was also announced at the draw that Hampden had been confirmed as the venue for the final on October 27th and the quarter-final ties were to be two-legged affairs on September 15th and 19th. Dundee United manager Willie MacFadyen watched the draw with interest to see if United's 'B' Division match against Queen's Park at Hampden on the 15th would have much competition for spectators from the League Cup games and also if their reserves would have Dundee to themselves for their 'C' Division match against Hibernian 'A' and in the event, he was happy with Dundee drawn away in the first leg.

Falkirk were managed by Bob Shankly who would famously lead Dundee to the Scottish League Championship eleven years later but now, in his first managerial job, he was plotting the downfall of The Dee. Falkirk's only other appearance in the League Cup quarter-final was in 1947/48 when, after beating Hamilton, they defeated Rangers in the semi before losing to East Fife in the final after a reply.

Before the Falkirk tie, Dundee opened their league campaign at Stirling Albion on Saturday 8th September and came away with a 2-2 draw thanks two goals from Ernie Copland in his only league appearance of the season. Billy Steel was missing again thanks to the injury picked up against Hearts in the penultimate sectional tie and he was a major doubt for the quarter-final in seven days time.

Still living in Glasgow, Steel asked Partick Thistle if he could train at Firhill on Wednesday afternoon in an effort to get fit and tested his ankle for the first time since Tynecastle. It didn't go well and the 'Pocket Dynamo' was still a major doubt for Saturday but he was still listed in the squad of twelve by George Anderson on the Friday.

Falkirk themselves had worries after they picked up injuries in the Dewar Shield semi-final win over St Johnstone on Wednesday. The Dewar Shield was competed for annually by the Aberdeenshire, Forfarshire, Perthshire and Stirlingshire Cup winners and after their win, which had been watched by Dundee trainer Reggie Smith, Bob Shankly said *"We weren't in top form against Saints but we are saving up the good shift for Dundee."*

The same day Dundee announced that the forthcoming Rangers game on September 29th was to be first all-ticket match of the season and prices for the stand were advertised at 6s, 5s and 4s, 3s for the stand enclosure and 1s 6d for the ground but the focus of the players was very much on Saturday's match at Brockville.

On the way to Brockville, the Dundee bus dropped the 'A' team off at Stirling for their 'C' Division match and as they were to kick off later, the first team were to wait outside Annfield in order to pick them up after the game.

Billy Steel wasn't on the bus as his ankle was still badly swollen and it was decided not to take the risk and play him but he made his own way to Brockville to lend his support from the stand.

For the opening ten minutes, Falkirk hammered Dundee and continued to bombard them for most of the match. It quickly turned into a superb rearguard action from The Dee and in Bill Brown a hero was found and his reputation was enhanced no end with his best display to date. He came off his line effectively, catching crosses time and time again and his handling was superb all afternoon. He dealt with everything Falkirk had to throw at him and was largely responsible for the match ending 0-0, with his understanding with Doug Cowie auguring well for the future.

The Falkirk crowd, which had the Scotland selectors in the stand, gave their players a rousing reception at the end but it was probably the men in dark blue (Falkirk played in their white change kit) who left the field the happiest to still be level in the tie.

Two days later on Monday 17th September, the Scottish League made the draw for the semi-finals of the League Cup, which was surprising considering that it was three days before the quarter-final second legs and a month before the penultimate round was due to be played.

The draw was kind to Dundee as it paired Dundee or Falkirk with St Johnstone or Motherwell and with 'Well 4-0 up after the first leg it Perth, it was likely to be the men from Fir Park should The Dark Blues dispose of The Bairns.

It meant that they had avoided the Old Firm with Celtic or Forfar Athletic drawing Dunfermline or Rangers. The potential Old Firm semi was to be played at Hampden while if Dundee reached the last four, their match would be at Ibrox.

There was more good news for Dundee when Doug Cowie was rewarded for his good performance at Brockville by being named as reserve for the Scottish League's match against the Irish League the following week, with Gerry Follon also named as a non travelling reserve. There was controversy with the squad however as there were no players from any east coast club in the starting eleven, but for Cowie it was a 'foot in the door' two years before he'd play for either the Scottish League or the full international side.

Come Wednesday, Dundee made three changes from the side that drew at Brockville with the most significant one being the return of Billy Steel at inside-right after passing a fitness test in the morning. George Hill came in to replace the injured Flavell after some good performances in the reserves while Ken Zeising came back in for Ernie Copland and the return of both Steel and Zeising were crucial in turning the tie Dundee's way with both goals in a tight 2-1 win.

Bob Shankly fielded the same eleven as the first leg, five of whom had played Junior football the year before and they were unlucky to lose their first game of the season. It was a purple patch in the closing fifteen minutes of the first half which won it for The Dee when they scored two great goals to send them into the semis and the majority of the 20,000 crowd home happy.

It was a typical cup-tie, with Falkirk refusing to admit defeat until the final whistle and for long periods The Bairns had the home defence worried with the forcing play of their wing-halves. The Falkirk threat was evident from the off and it was no surprise when they opened the scoring through Mochan in twenty-four minutes when Dundee were temporarily down to ten men due to an injury to Gordon Frew.

It was the return of Frew on the half hour that was the signal for a spell of Dundee pressure and on thirty-four minutes they got themselves back on level terms. After Dundee's fifth corner in a row, the ball was cleared to Andy Irvine who pushed a ball through the centre and with Zeising nipping in between two Falkirk defenders, he cracked the ball into the net.

Dundee were rampant now and Steel was jinking about in grand style and five minutes later he combined with George Christie for what proved to be the winner. Billy took a throw-in on the left and gave it to Christie who proceeded to beat the full-back and cut inside. As he approached another defender, Christie stepped aside and left it for Steel who took it in his stride, beat two men on the run and gave Scott in The Bairns' goal not an earthly with a low shot.

The second half was end to end with Bill Brown producing a string of good saves, just as he had done in the first leg, while Doug Cowie had to clear one off the line from Plumb in the dying minutes and it was a relieved George Anderson who faced the press after the 2-1 win. Appearing in a cheerful mood he joked, *"I think we can beat Celtic in the Final all right,"* but this seemed a little premature after Rangers had overturned a 1-0 first leg deficit to Dunfermline with a 3-1 win at Ibrox.

Celtic had drawn 1-1 at Forfar to go through 5-2 on aggregate to set up the Old Firm semi while Motherwell beat St Johnstone 3-0 at Fir Park for a 7-0 aggregate win and they could now look forward to a semi-final with Dundee at Ibrox on Saturday 13th October.

Despite Anderson's confidence that Dundee would reach their first League Cup Final, Motherwell would be no pushovers and were in fact the holders after beating Hibernian and their 'Famous Five' forward line 3-0 in the final twelve months previously.

Two weeks before the semi-final, Dundee had a superb 1-0 win over Rangers in front of 31,000 at Dens but it was a victory at a price. Billy Steel had been the match winner with the only goal but he injured his ankle again and missed the next match against Hearts at Tynecastle, seven days before the Motherwell game, as well as Scotland's international with Northern Ireland in Belfast.

Three days later, on Tuesday 9th October, trainer Reggie Smith spent an anxious day waiting for Steel to come through from Glasgow for special treatment on his ankle and he waited at Dens until 7.30pm. Smith had sent one of the trainees to pick him up from the station and when he didn't appear on any of the Glasgow trains during his eight-hour wait at Dundee West, Smith then sent the trainee to check if Steel was at the hotel he normally stayed at in the city. When he wasn't there, Smith, in a panic, managed to get a hold of Mrs Steel on the telephone who thought Billy didn't have to report to Dens until Wednesday but didn't know where he was!

Billy did turn up on Wednesday morning however when he did a spot of training on his own before going off to watch his team mates in the afternoon, taking on the Dundee City Police in a golf competition at Downfield. The players took a break from training to play six four-ball foursomes with the local constabulary and when Dundee FC won 5-1, captain Alfie Boyd suggested it should be an annual event at the post-match banquet.

Steel wasn't the only doubt for the semi as George Hill was struggling when he pulled a muscle in training and his left leg became swollen. In the end he missed out, with Toner switching to outside-right and Pattillo restored to the number eight jersey while Jack Cowan had recovered from injury and replaced Gordon Frew at left-back after having an excellent game against Celtic reserves last week.

The news that all Dundee fans wanted to know however was would their hero Billy Steel be fit and, after working on his ankle on Thursday, *The Evening Telegraph* declared on their front page on Friday that he was fit and be among the thirteen travelling to Glasgow; much to the relief of all concerned in dark blue.

The Sunday Post referred to the Dundee-Motherwell semi-final as *'an all time classic'* but it is unlikely anyone in claret and amber would agree as Dundee ran out 5-1 winners. It had all the thrills of a knock-out battle, performed as *The Sporting Post* put it *'in masterly style'* and for Dundee, their movement was *'silky and intelligent and a joy to watch'*.

A big factor in Dundee's victory was the performance of Bobby Flavell, who was returned to his place in the centre after a spell on the wing and the move paid dividends with a superb performance. The Flavell-Steel combination paid off handsomely with Steel setting up four of the goals but it was Bobby who grabbed the headlines, proving a deadly finisher with a well-earned hat-trick.

The game was much tighter than the score suggested however when, after leading 2-1 in a thrilling first half (with goals from Christie and Flavell), the second period saw the Dark Blues come under intense pressure as Motherwell sought to draw level. However, with nineteen minutes remaining Pattillo grabbed a third before Flavell added another two near the end to give The Dark Blues a rather flattering 5-1 scoreline.

Dundee weren't complaining however as they were through to their first national final since 1925. George Anderson was understandably buoyant at full time, shaking the hand of every player as they left the park before predicting that Dundee would lift the trophy on October 27th.

He had previously told the press not to be surprised by what Dundee might do in this competition once they were out the group stages and so few could now argue with him that his side might continue to surprise when the final came around.

Chapter 12:
Alfie Boyd

FROM BALL BOY to net boy, to the captain with the most winners' medals in Dundee's history, Alfie Boyd can truly lay claim to the worthy mantle of Dundee legend, having played for the Dark Blues for six successful years in the late Forties and early Fifties.

Born in the city on October 22nd 1920, Alfred Boyd started his connection with the club as a ball boy in the Roaring Twenties before being promoted to the prestigious position of net boy. With football coursing through his veins however, he was destined to become a player and the first signs of his exceptional talent came when he played in a 1-0 victory for the Scottish Schoolboys over their English counterparts in Newcastle in 1935.

Within three years of that cap, Alfie started his senior career not in his home town but up the river in Perth when he signed for St. Johnstone, but like so many players of his era his career was curtailed by the Second World War, when he joined the R.A.F. and was posted to South Africa.

At the end of the war, Boyd was stationed at Leuchars before he was demobbed, allowing him to rekindle his football career with the Saints but in February 1947 he was tempted to join Dundee by the Dark Blues' managing/director George Anderson who parted with a Dens Park club record fee of £4,000 to secure his services.

Within weeks of Alfie joining, Dundee chalked up back to back club record 10-0 wins over Alloa and Dunfermline and by the end of the season were 'B' Division Champions for the second year in a row. This time Dundee were allowed back into the top tier with promotion being resumed after the war for the first time and the Dark Blues were back in the big time.

In his six years at Dens, Alfie would miss only six games which is a remarkable record and is a testimony to his peak physical fitness. As a centre half or wing half, he formed part of the famous half-back line of Gallagher, Cowie and Boyd and played no fewer than 235 games for the Dee, scoring twenty-seven times.

Season 1948/49 was the nearly season in so many ways as Dundee reached the semi-final of both the League Cup and Scottish Cup and finished runners-up in the League Championship after a last day 4-0 collapse at Falkirk, where a win would have guaranteed the League flag.

Those defeats hurt Alfie and in a newspaper interview in 1950 he stated, "We had to win our last four games to be Champions but we were inclined to be too much on edge. In our last match with Falkirk at Brockville, a win would have made us Champions, but everything went wrong. We were all over them in the first half, but when Alec Stott failed with a penalty close on half time, we felt that the fates were against us.

"We got into the semi-final of both the League Cup and Scottish Cup and I think our defeat by Clyde in the replay of the Scottish was as hard a blow as any. We had gone to Tynecastle in the round before the semi and won handsomely. I had visions of a Cup medal, the one thing we all dream of winning, but Clyde put an end to that dream."

It was during this time that Alfie won his only international honour, playing for the Scottish League against the English League in 1949 and at the start of the following season took both the Scottish and English Trainers and Players coaching course, becoming the first player to complete both in Britain. While undertaking the Scottish certificate, he studied on the course with such luminaries as Jock Stein, Willie Ormond and Reggie Smith as well as Sammy Kean, who would be part of Dundee's backroom staff when they won the League in 1962.

In an effort to win their first honour since 1910, Dundee splashed out a world record transfer fee for Billy Steel in September 1950. Dundee then finished in third place, behind Rangers on goal average and Alfie surprisingly finished Dundee's top goalscorer that season with eight goals before also becoming the Dundee F.C. cricket team's top batsman in the summer, scoring forty runs in a match against Forfarshire Cricket Club.

It wasn't long however before Alfie achieved his dream of a winner's medal when, in October 1951, Dundee ended their wait for silverware with a 3-2 League Cup Final win over Rangers at Hampden.

In front of 92,325 at the national stadium, Dundee were leading 2-1 with only minutes left on the clock but unfortunately for The Dee, Rangers equalised in controversial fashion when Dundee keeper Bill Brown looked to have been fouled by Willie Thornton.

From the restart however, Dundee won a free kick deep inside the Rangers half and with only seconds remaining, Billy Steel is reputed to have said to his skipper, "I'll place it on your head Alfie," and did just that as Boyd headed home the winner.

It was one of the most fantastic finishes ever seen at Hampden and Boyd held aloft the glittering League Cup before the ecstatic Dundonians in the crowd.

Later that season Alfie led Dundee back to Hampden for the Scottish Cup Final in April and in October 1952, Dundee made it three trips to Hampden in a year to defend their League Cup trophy.

This time they faced 'B' Division Kilmarnock, and two goals from Bobby Flavell was enough to let Alfie get the chance to lift the trophy for a second time as Dundee became the first side to retain the League Cup.

At the end of the following season, Dundee went on a marathon two-month tour of South Africa as part of the club's sixtieth anniversary celebrations and at the end of the tour, Dundee granted Boyd permission to remain in South Africa. Alfie had enjoyed his time in South Africa during the war where he met his wife and now wished to return to her homeland where his daughter was born and signed for the Marist Brothers Club as player/coach.

Aflie turned down the chance to rejoin Dundee in 1957 as by then he was involved in the South African gold mining industry. He would go on to manage Durban City and manage a Sir Stanley Matthews Invitation XI during one of the Englishman's many visits to the continent and he also became a selector for the South African F.A.

Alfie however kept in touch with many of his team mates from Dens and in 1993 returned to the city to take part in Dundee's centenary celebrations and catch up with many old friends and colleagues.

Alfie sadly passed away in South Africa in July 1998 aged 78 and did so just a few weeks after sending Dundee a congratulatory message on winning promotion back to the Scottish Premier League. From having been a ball boy at Dens at a young age, Dundee was in his heart until the end and he will forever be remembered as the legendary double cup winning captain who led by example and scored that famous last minute winner.

Honours at Dundee:

Scottish League Cup winners:	1951/52, 1952/53
Scottish League Championship runners-up:	1948/49
Scottish Cup runners-up:	1952
Scottish League B Division champions:	1946/47
Scottish League cap:	1

Appearances, Goals:

League:	169, 18 goals
Scottish Cup:	21, 3 goals
League Cup:	44, 6 goals
Totals:	235, 27 goals

Chapter 13:
"On Your Head, Alfie"

DUNDEE FOOTBALL CLUB were into their first ever League Cup Final on Saturday 27th October 1951 and their opponents would be Rangers after they had defeated Celtic 3-0 in the semis. Rangers, by contrast, considered the trophy almost their own, having won the Southern League Cup and the Scottish League Cup six times before and were desperate to get it back after two years without a victory.

The omens didn't look good for The Dee as not only did Rangers have a great cup record but Dundee had a poor one at Hampden having never won not only a final there but also a semi-final. They had lost in Mount Florida on five occasions with Dundee's only ever major final success taking place at Ibrox in 1910.

However, the Dundee players had a quiet confidence about them in the lead-up to the big day as they had not only defeated Rangers just before the semi-final but had also beaten Celtic 2-1 at Dens in the only match between the semi and the final. A crowd of 32,000, Dundee's highest home league attendance of the season, gave the Dark Blues a good send off before the final and the players responded in kind with goals from Christie and Pattillo to secure an Old Firm league double.

The fans had also snapped up cup final stand tickets in double quick time when they went on sale three days after the semi with prices being set at 21s, 10s 6d, 7s 6d and 5s. Applications were invited for Dundee's allocation by post with money and a stamped addressed envelope to be sent to the secretary's address in Reform Street and after an unprecedented demand for tickets they had to return some stamped envelopes with the cash intact and an apology.

Dundee had asked the Scottish League for extra tickets but were told that there were none left and in a press release the League said, *"We are surprised by the demand which has been a bigger rush than for the Old Firm."* They also said that the official crowd for the Dundee v Motherwell semi-final had been bizarrely increased from the originally announced 25,000 to 31,000 which was significant as the revenues from both semis were pooled between the four participating clubs.

For those unfortunate enough not to get a stand ticket, there wasn't really a problem as it was announced that the enclosures were pay at the gate and an estimated 30,000 Dundonians were expected to make the trip west. Around 10,000 of them were expected to travel on six football special trains on Saturday morning from Dundee West station to Glasgow leaving at 8.35am, 9.30am, 9.45am, 10.38am, 11.00am and 11.22am and at a price of 11s 6d for a return, tickets had to be booked in advance. (Six trains were to return home from Buchanan Street station between 6.00pm and 7.50pm with a provision being made in the event of extra time).

A further 6,000 were expected to travel by bus when it emerged that a huge number of coaches had been booked. Many had made provisional bookings before the semi-final and since the Motherwell game, bus proprietors were deluged with enquires for the final.

W. Alexander and Son Ltd had bookings for an incredible 135 coaches and had to call in many buses from outlying depots of other companies. A. W. Watson & Co. advertised six 'football specials' while Dickson's Coaches had thirty-five buses booked with enquires for their buses starting as early as 8am on the Sunday after the semi at the home of the Dickson's manager.

The League Cup Final really looked to have captured the imagination of the Dark Blue public and in Glasgow interest was high when the Scottish League put their allocation of stand tickets on sale on Tuesday 23rd October. They were swamped in the early part of the day and their tickets sold out by early evening. When Dundee learned about the sale, they complained to the League as they had asked for extra briefs and been told there were none and said that selling these in Glasgow meant most would have gone to Rangers' fans. These protests however fell on deaf ears.

Billy Steel played in the win over Celtic on October 20th but was struggling with the ankle injury which would trouble him for the rest of his career. He trained on his own at Firhill on the Monday and then declared himself fit for the final and there was a collective sigh of relief at Dens which Billy could probably have heard from Maryhill.

On the Tuesday before the Celtic game however, Steel had to appear in front of the The Referee and Rough Play Committee at the S.F.A.'s headquarters in Glasgow. He was called to answer accusations made against him by the referee at the Austria v Scotland match in June, where Billy became the first Scottish player to be sent off and, although the case had already been discussed by the SFA, they wanted to hear what he had to say on the matter.

The meeting lasted half an hour and after listening to Steel and reading the official report from F.I.F.A., it was decided that no further action was necessary. George Anderson had travelled down from Aberdeen to accompany Steel to Park Gardens, although he wasn't allowed into the meeting. After the verdict was announced, Anderson told the *Glasgow Evening Times* that, *"It is hardly the perfect build up to two huge games for the club but I am pleased for Billy that the matter is now closed."*

Having declared himself fit however, Steel could concentrate on the cup final build-up but there were others in the Dundee squad who were struggling to make the big day. Bill Brown had been limping at the end of the Celtic game, Doug Cowie also took a knock but said he would be fine as did Alfie Boyd, who hadn't been risked against the Parkhead side in an effort to make sure he was ready for Hampden.

After changing the players' routine in the build-up to Brockville in 1949, Anderson decided to have no special training at Dens and to just have a week of normal routine with the only change being that the squad were to travel through to Glasgow on Friday afternoon on the 3pm train.

Anderson also arranged for a special carriage for the players to be added to the homeward bound train on Saturday because they had had to travel back in the guard's van after the semi-final. The players' wives were also officially invited to attend but would be travelling through on their own on Saturday morning.

The players were in relaxed mood though and on the Tuesday played the final round of the Dens Park club's annual golf medal which was won by Ken Zeising. The award, a handsome gold and enamel affair, was awarded to the player with the best aggregate of three net scores and, after the first two rounds were played at Downfield earlier in the season, the final lap was played on the Carnoustie Championship course.

Zeising began with a two-round total of 155, one stroke ahead of last year's winner Doug Cowie and club captain Alfie Boyd and after a round of 81, with a two-stroke handicap taking it down to 79, his aggregate of 234 made Ken the winner, eight stokes ahead of his nearest rival.

Doug Cowie was second (89 – 3 for 86, aggregate 242) and Tommy Gallacher third (91 – 14 for 77, aggregate 244) and the prizes were presented by manager George Anderson at a tea at the Bruce Hotel.

Anderson himself was in jovial mood telling Rueben Bennett that he was the only one who took training seriously when he came off the last green carrying his own clubs while the rest of the squad used caddie cars. He also joked with George Christie when he saw the winger had a three-figure score that he thought football was the only game Christie couldn't play and the enjoyable day put the final to the back of everyone's minds.

The players were re-focused twenty-four hours later when all of Dundee's squad were in full training, including Steel and Cowie. Cowie trained with a small plaster on the leg knocked against Celtic but he was kicking the ball without any jarring effect. The only real defensive selection issue for Anderson was whether to play Jack Cowan or Gordon Frew at left-back as both men were fit for the first time that season.

George Hill was struggling however and it looked increasingly likely that the same forward line that had played the past two matches would be the one to line up at Hampden, namely that of Toner-Pattillo-Flavell-Steel-Christie. This led to *The Courier* debating the merits of playing Jimmy Toner out of position but Anderson was quick to defend his player by telling reporter Colin Glen, *"Jimmy Toner is a polished player and I hold that, in present day football, such a man can make his presence felt in any position."*

Anderson was a master of man-management, a master of publicity and a master also of pre-match psychology with the opposition, forty or fifty years before Sir Alex Ferguson was attributed to have invented such a thing and on the eve of the final, he was up to his tricks with Rangers in an attempt to gain some sort of advantage.

On Wednesday, Anderson was on the phone to the Scottish League saying that he was willing for Rangers to play in their customary light blue with Dundee in their change colours of white and the League said they would pass his suggestion on to Ibrox. The rule in the League Cup was that if the colours of both teams clashed, then both teams had to change but Rangers were delighted to accept Dundee's suggestion and announced their gratitude to Mr. Anderson and Dundee. They also said that they would play in a popular light blue shirt with two bands of red across the middle that they last wore in a cup tie against Raith Rovers two years before.

Rangers manager Bill Struth personally phoned Anderson to thank him and also asked him if the Dens Park chief could return any unsold stand tickets. *"Ours sold out long before yours,"* Anderson told him, *"But you can have one of mine for a guinea if you like?"*

Anderson knew exactly what he was doing as he knew it would be a popular move with both Rangers and Dundee fans alike. There was a glamour to the light blue jerseys which made Rangers a big appeal but he also thought that Dundee looked slick in their white shirts with a dark blue collar and cuffs and that his players would stand out on front of the huge anticipated crowd at Hampden.

Rangers themselves were doing no special training and on Wednesday went to Troon for a day's golf which was a regular part of their training. Rangers' part-time players weren't there as the likes of Cox, Brown, McColl and Thornton were sticking to their Tuesday and Thursday evening sessions at Ibrox and Struth announced it was, *"Business as usual."*

He also said that the Light Blues wouldn't announce their team before Thursday at the earliest but it was suspected that the eleven who had played against Celtic in the semi and subsequently in a floodlit friendly against Arsenal at Highbury and Hearts in the league would be the eleven for the final.

In the build-up, the players were in demand for interviews with newspapers and in *The Scotsman* Tommy Gallacher said that he was looking to make his name at Hampden just as his father had done against The Dark Blues in the Scottish Cup Final in 1925. Patsy Gallacher got the winner that day in a 2-1 win and they also interviewed Dundee's goalscorer that day, Davie McLean, who said that Gallacher *"Makes the mazy runs like his father used to do,"* and was sure he would follow in his father's cup winning footsteps.

Billy Steel told *The Evening Telegraph* that he was desperate to win as he'd never won a cup final before while Jimmy Toner said he was hoping to add a League Cup winners' medal to his Scottish Junior Cup one and there was no doubt that the Dundee players were extremely motivated.

The same week saw the 1951 General Election held in Great Britain and when the results came through, the Conservatives won with Winston Churchill regaining Number 10 from Clement Atlee, having lost to Labour five years before. Churchill had no love for Dundee however after it voted him out in the General Election of 1922 in favour of Prohibitionist Neddy Scrymgeour.

Churchill was elected as a Liberal MP for the city in 1908 and initially saw Dundee as *"A seat for life,"* but suffered the inconvenience of it being 440 miles from Westminster. In those days, Dundee was only practically accessible by a rather joyless, overnight sleeper train from King's Cross and Scotland's third largest city was hardly a joyful place in which to arrive of a morning, dark, tall and grimy, with much unemployment, poverty and drunkenness.

Curiously, the electorate at first felt honoured to be represented by a Cabinet minister and seemed prepared to overlook Churchill's long absences, but the relationship became strained after World War One, when Churchill's own controversial escapades, compounded with much local bitterness and disillusionment, led to his defeat in 1922. He finished fourth behind Scrymgeour and later wrote: *"I found myself without an office, without a seat, without a party and without an appendix. I may never be able forgive Dundee,"* while his friend T.E. Lawrence said, *"What bloody shits the Dundeans must be."* There was every chance therefore that the new Prime Minister would be supporting Rangers in the League Cup Final.

Rangers themselves were treating it as a home game with the same matchday routines as a game at Ibrox, including having lunch in their usual hotel.

Dundee were staying in a Glasgow city centre hotel just a hundred yards from Buchanan Street Station and, after arriving early evening, they went for a meal before going to bed at 10.30pm.

In the morning the players were deliberately late in getting up before having a short walk and then breakfast and left for Hampden on a private coach at 12.30pm. They arrived at the National Stadium just after 1pm, ninety minutes before kick off and already there were plenty of Dundee fans milling about. The kick off was set for 2.30pm in case extra time was needed as Hampden didn't yet have floodlights and those who had arrived on the early football specials were already there to welcome the team off the bus.

The match referee for the final was one of Scotland's foremost officials Jack Mowat. Mowat was a first class referee from 1946 until 1960 when he was in charge of the famous Real Madrid v Eintracht Frankfurt European Cup Final at Hampden in his final game. Born in Rutherglen on April 1st 1908, Mowat would referee one match at the 1958 World Cup Finals as well as seven Scottish Cup finals and the 1951 Scottish League Cup final, his first.

Dundee's line-up for the big day was (with position in brackets) : Bill Brown (gk), Gerry Follon (rb), Jack Cowan (lb), Tommy Gallacher (rh), Doug Cowie (ch), Alfie Boyd (lh) capt., Jimmy Toner (rw), Johnny Pattillo (ir), Bobby Flavell (cf), Billy Steel (il), George Christie (lw).

The Rangers side, which included eight full internationalist, was: Bobby Brown (gk), George Young (rb) capt., John Little (lb), Ian McColl (rh), Willie Woodburn (ch), Sammy Cox (lh), Willie Waddell (rw), Willie Findlay (ir), Willie Thornton (cf), Joe Johnson (il), Eddie Rutherford (lw).

George Young won the toss and much to the relief of Dens skipper Alfie Boyd, chose to attack the traditional 'Rangers end' (the covered west enclosure to the left of the old South Stand as you look at the pitch) – relief because Dundee had kicked that way in the opening half in their two unsuccessful semi-finals in season 1948/49.

Dundee therefore kicked off and in the opening fifteen minutes were in control with Billy Steel spraying passes all over the field. Dundee were well on top with the line of 'wee fellas' that the

Dundee forward line were nicknamed, having the towering Rangers defence in a whirl. The Dens Park forward line was probably the lightest in the country but in skill, nimbleness, fight and poise they often showed they had few equals and they started the cup final in great fettle.

Steel at times was lying very deep but was effective in playing long through passes to Christie that had McColl and Young repeatedly worried. On the other wing, the twists and turns of Flavell, with his precise flicks, were a constant worry to Woodburn, while Pattillo's roaming and sudden bursts and Toner's neat ball control and occasional rambles into the middle were a source of delight to the Dundee fans and kept the Light Blues' defence on edge.

It all looked to be going to plan and only to be a matter of time until Dundee scored but as is so often the case in football the opposite happened when Willie Findlay put Rangers ahead on twenty-one minutes against the run of play.

The goal really knocked Dundee's stride and the men from Govan started to take command. Alfie Boyd had played as almost a second centre-half and with Billy Steel still lying deep, Dundee's long ball tactics made little impression on Rangers' 'Iron Curtain' defence. The second phase of the first half saw Dundee have a tendency to sky the ball forward which suited the hefty Rangers back line. At half time The Dark Blues regrouped and discussed placing an emphasis on short passing along the ground to draw out the Ibrox defence.

Immediately this philosophy paid dividends as Dundee drew level two minutes into the second half when the ever-alert Flavell fired Christie's cross into the net despite the best efforts of Bobby Brown.

From now on Dundee were terrific with their mid-line dominant. There was Tommy Gallacher holding the ball, beating his man and pushing through the perfect ground passes; there was Doug Cowie as firm as a rock, thwarting Thornton at every turn and Alfie Boyd, the inspired skipper, back in defence when required and putting a check on Willie Waddell when needed, whom Jack Cowan was finding quite a handful.

Cowan in general had a tough afternoon saying post match that he, *"found Waddell six times faster that the last time I played him."* The Canadian however played the Rangers flier with grit, determination and courage and was on hand to clear off the line at 1-1. He played his part in going into attack at the right time and it was his clearance which led to Dundee's second.

On sixty-nine minutes, Cowan cleared the ball from the box and the ball went to Flavell, who passed it on with a dainty flick. Johnny Pattillo came steaming in and he hit Bobby's pass on the run; a beauty which flew into the Rangers' net to give Dundee a 2-1 lead.

Rangers tried to push on and rescue the tie but they found Bill Brown in tremendous form whom *The Courier* said *"rose to the occasion like a veteran."* Gerry Follon also rose to the occasion after a shaky start and prevented the sturdy Johnson and the eager Rutherford from getting into their stride and as the game wore on, it looked like the Dark Blues might just hold on for victory.

With two minutes left however, disaster struck when Rangers drew level in controversial circumstances. George Young took a free kick just inside the Dundee half and floated it into the Dark Blues' box and when Bill Brown went up to catch it, he was nudged by Willie Thornton and the ball floated into the net.

Dundee were furious and Brown chased Mowat shouting, *"He pushed me ref, he pushed me!"* while Alfie Boyd also protested, but the referee was well-placed and paid no heed to the appeals.

There was some doubt as to whether the future Dundee boss Thornton had touched it or whether it was George Young's goal but Rangers didn't care as it looked like they had forced extra time.

From the restart however Billy Steel was fouled just inside the Rangers' half and Dundee had one last chance to grab a winner. With just thirty seconds remaining, Steel placed the ball on the ground, preparing to take the kick and as he did so, Alfie Boyd sped past him saying, *"I'm going to the right of* the goal so try to chip the ball over to me."

"*I'll place it on your head, Alfie,*" Steel replied as he was teeing up the ball and when he took the free kick, he did exactly that, dropping it to Boyd eight yards out. Boyd leapt up, closed his eyes and headed it for all it was worth and when he opened his eyes the ball was in the back of the net to win the League Cup for Dundee.

Alfie was swamped by his joyous team mates, while Steel just gave his skipper a wink and when Rangers re-started the match, the final whistle immediately blew and Dundee had won the match 3-2.

It was one of the most dramatic finishes ever seen in a Hampden final and the 30,000 Dundonians in the crowd, many of whom had gathered on the terracing below the North Stand, let out a tremendous roar when the game was won. Dundee were the League Cup winners for the first time and a new generation of Dees had finally seen the Dark Blues win some silverware after a forty-one year wait.

A delirious George Anderson ran onto the pitch and congratulated each and every one of the victorious Dark Blues before Scottish League president John McMahon presented the beautiful trophy to Alfie Boyd on the pitch. Boyd was lifted up by Tommy Gallacher and Billy Steel and the skipper held aloft the glittering trophy for all to see.

"*It was a wonderful moment,*" recalled Doug Cowie in Norrie Price's book, *Up Wi' The Bonnets!* "*It was a great game but I felt we had the edge and deserved to win.*"

It had been a great team performance and Steel had been an inspiration and many believed that the bigger the occasion, the better he played and he certainly proved that theory that afternoon.

The plaudits came rolling in with Tommy Gallacher's father Patsy leading them saying, "*It was a grand game; one of the best I've ever watched. Before the game I said if Dundee kept the ball on the ground they would win and they did. They were terrific and I was of course very pleased with the way Tommy played!*"

Scottish League secretary Fred Denovan said that it was, "*The best League Cup Final we've ever seen and a truly great game!*" The League were delighted with not only the final but also the whole tournament which had been a big success in terms of crowds and entertainment and the final's crowd of 92,325 was the highest League Cup Final attendance to date. It was a crowd that would not be bettered in League Cup terms for twelve years until 105,907 would turn up to watch Rangers beat Morton in October 1963 and is today still the fourth biggest crowd in League Cup history, with the top two being for Old Firm Finals in 1965 and 1970.

George Anderson said it was a dream come true and told the *Dundee Courier* that, "*We have planned and re-planned until now we can say we almost have the ideal team. We gave a display in the very highest of Scottish traditions. While I thank the players for their performance, I also want to say that we owe a great deal to the work of Reggie Smith and Reuben Bennett in training the players. It was a real club effort.*"

To emphasis a club ethos that the modern day fans' owned club would be proud of was highlighted by the experience of Dundee's young reserve Archie Simpson who was currently stationed in Edinburgh doing his National Service with the Highland Light Infantry. Archie had hitch-hiked through from the capital with a Dundee supporting friend to support their team and when Anderson spotted them on the terracing he invited them both to the dressing room at the end of the match.

Archie started to help Reggie Smith clear up the dressing room, just as he would have done as an apprentice at Dens but Anderson stopped him and told him that is not why he was invited in and told to drink some champagne from the cup as well as offering the same to his star struck friend! He then gave the pair a lift back to the train station on the team coach and paid for their train tickets back to Edinburgh.

Before they left Hampden, Anderson received telegrams of congratulations from Washington, Calcutta and Paris as well as from all over the country. He also heard from Dundee Lord Provost Fenton who was visiting boarded-out children in the north of Scotland, Mr Ebbe Schwartz, President of the Danish FA and Mr Otto Simecheck, who had arranged the summer tour of Israel, while *The Sunday Post* reported that the biggest cheer of the day at Pittodrie had been when they heard news of Dundee's victory.

The Dundee party got a great send-off from Glasgow where thousands packed Buchanan Street Station and the crowds were so big that the wives of Billy Steel and Bobby Flavell got separated from the rest of the group. The police had to force a way through for them and when they arrived at the train, Mrs Flavell had a sprained ankle and damaged nylons, for which George Anderson promised to buy her a new pair.

Alfie Boyd, who was carrying the cup, was carried shoulder high with Steel, Flavell, Follon and Brown also hoisted aloft and when Boyd got into the train he continued to wave the trophy at the supporters through the carriage window. The train eventually got underway just after 6pm with the platform still thronging with Dees, but it was nothing to the number of fans they would encounter upon returning to Juteopolis.

Ninety minutes before the train was due into Dundee, the crowds began to gather outside Dundee West Station, the site of the modern day city centre station. Forty policemen were reinforced with nightshift men and railway police who tried to keep the station clear and by a quirk of fate the policeman on duty at the main door was Mr James Golden of Lochee, who was the same policeman guarding the same door when Dundee returned with the Scottish Cup in 1910.

The supporters who arrived on the players' train made a cheering lane through which Alfie Boyd, still carrying the cup, had to force his way to Yeaman Shore where they met a bus to take them on a tour of the city. The bus was filled with players and their wives and officials of the club, including managing-director Anderson and chairman James Gellatly and Boyd and others climbed on top of the roof to take the acclaim of the city.

The Hampden roar came to Dundee as the bus, preceded by a police wireless car, moved off towards South Union Street. Boyd and his team mates, perched dangerously on the roof, holding the trophy up high, were cheered as the bus made its way at a snail's pace round Whitehall Crescent into Dock Street and back towards South Union Street.

Policemen were swept aside in the melee as the bus crawled up Union Street to the High Street and traffic in the High Street and Reform Street came to a standstill as the bus drove round the City Square. There were incredible scenes in the city centre with an estimated 20,000 out to hail their heroes and people were held up in ten trams while cars were abandoned and stranded in the middle of the road.

Fifteen policemen surrounded the bus until the crowd thinned out before it drove to the chairman's house in West Ferry, where the cup was once again filled with champagne. Mr Gellatly thanked the team for their great performance while Anderson said he had a big 'thank you' to say to the players and Alfie Boyd responded for the players saying that they were all proud to play for Dundee and wanted to thank Anderson and particularly Bennett and Smith, the trainers, for getting them so fit.

After the players' late supper, Johnny Pattillo drove Anderson and his party back to Aberdeen in director Jack Swadel's car before returning the car in the morning when he and Alfie Boyd headed north again in his own car for a training session with kids in the Granite City on Sunday night.

It was a night of revelry in Dundee reminiscent of V.E. Day six years before and not seen in footballing terms for over four decades. Many public houses ignored their closing times to which the police turned a blind eye, with Alfie Boyd, Billy Steel, George Anderson & Co. the toast of the city. It was in a night of never-to-be forgotten celebration as Dundee hailed their first ever Hampden Heroes and there was real hope that the Dark Blues could build on the remarkable success.

Chapter 14:
Jimmy Toner

JIMMY TONER IS one of a unique group of players who won two major winners medals with Dundee when he was part of the sides to win back to back Scottish League Cups in the early Fifties.

Born on August 23rd 1924, Jimmy served in the Second World War when he played for his regiment side and his football career kicked off properly at the end of the conflict when he joined Junior side Fauldhouse United.

A couple of years later he signed for The Dark Blues and made his debut for Dundee on Christmas Eve 1949 when he scored a double in a home win against Stirling Albion. The following week at Ibrox he scored again in a 2-2 draw but that wasn't the first time Jimmy had been hitting the headlines. His time at Fauldhouse United saw him enjoy some major success, winning the Scottish Junior Cup and he scored a goal in the final that was described by the *Daily Express* as *"One of the most amazing goals ever seen at Hampden Park."*

"I was playing for my works team at the time when I was spotted by a scout from Fauldhouse," recalls Jimmy, *"And he asked me to play for them at the start of 1945. My signing on fee for them was a new pair of boots and five pounds.*

"I played in the Junior Cup Final against Arthurlie before joining Dundee where my goal was described in the papers as one of the best ever seen at Hampden. I picked the ball up on my eighteen-yard line and ran the length of the pitch, beating four defenders. I stumbled and just managed to keep my feet and get a shot in and luckily for us it went in."

Fauldhouse beat Arthurlie 2-0 in the 1945/46 Final and Jimmy remembers the crowds being huge throughout that victorious cup run.

"During that cup run we played Blantyre Vics in the quarter-final at Shawfield and they had to close the gates well before kick-off. People therefore started to climb up onto the enclosure roof to get a view but unfortunately someone fell through the roof and died.

"One thing that sticks in my mind is the crowds that came to watch the games in the latter stages. We played Blantyre Celtic in the semi-final and Arthurlie in the final and both games amassed a total of 75,000 people. Fauldhouse were a good football team and we went unbeaten for fifty-two games and won everything that year."

After that successful cup run, Jimmy was courted by some very big clubs but he joined Dundee after being recommended to Dark Blues' boss George Anderson by future Dee manager Bobby Ancell whom he met during the war.

"Not long after winning the Junior Cup, I signed for Dundee after saying no to Newcastle United, Manchester United and Burnley, who had just lost the FA Cup Final. Bobby Ancell and I played in the same team during the war and he recommended me to George Anderson. George had given me tickets for Burnley's cup final defeat to Charlton as well as to an international where I saw Billy Steel play for the first time. Little did I know I'd be his team mate in a few years' time and score on his Dundee debut.

"When I signed for Dundee I was still in the army and the club were giving me two pounds a week to play for them and I ended up at Dens Park for seven years."

As an inside-forward, Toner made seventy-one appearances for The Dee, scoring twenty-two times and his undoubted highlights were the two League Cup wins in 1951 and 1952. Jimmy played in the 3-2 win at Hampden over Rangers in October 1951 and twelve months later he was one of seven survivors from that game to win their second medal in the 2-0 win over Kilmarnock.

He scored five goals on the 'Road to Hampden' in 1951, all in the sectional ties, which included a hat-trick against Raith Rovers at Dens, while the following year he got another two goals en route to the final, against Airdrie at home and Clyde away in the group stages.

Dundee made it three finals within a year when they also played in the 1952 Scottish Cup Final against Motherwell but unfortunately lost 4-0 and Jimmy missed out on a hat-trick of appearances at the National Stadium due to injury.

"Unfortunately for me I was injured for the Cup Final against Motherwell but I was taken along by the club as a gesture and watched that game from the enclosure behind the dug-outs. I'm not a good spectator and it was murder to watch!

"Before that I played in that first League Cup Final against Rangers and that was another game where they had closed the gates. Funnily enough the Rangers inside-left was Joe Johnston who had played against me in the Junior Cup Final and he must have been sick of the sight of me.

"It was a terrible day as it had been raining and the Rangers players for me were a lot bigger than us. When they scored with a minute to go, it looked of course as if extra time was looming. The ball had glanced in off of Billy Brown's knuckles and my thought was that, due to it raining so much, our tops and our boots weighed down so heavily and as the Rangers players were a lot bigger than us, I thought we'd get murdered.

"Thankfully, however, we went straight back up the park and scored after winning a free kick from the kick-off. In those days, you gave the ball to the inside right from kick-off and he was fouled and from that free kick, Billy Steel put the ball straight onto Alfie Boyd's head for the winner. It was a brilliant occasion and when we got back to Dundee that night, the crowds were just magic!

"The next final the year after was the luckiest one I had been in as Kilmarnock were a very good side, despite being in the 'B' Division and played very well that day. They marked Billy Steel out the game but I set up Bobby Flavell's first ten minutes from time and then he scored another with a volley a few minutes later. I am very proud of the fact I won two cup winners' medals with Dundee and there are some great players in the club's history who can't say that."

Jimmy's time at Dens came to an end in 1954 when he joined Leeds United and, having played with one superstar, Billy Steel at Dens, he now joined up with another, John Charles at Elland Road.

"Leeds were in the Second Division at the time and were managed by Raich Carter who was a brilliant player in his day and played alongside Stanley Matthews for England. I also had the luck to play alongside John Charles, the famous Welsh international and he was the first British player to move to Italy when he joined Juventus. He was really admired over there.

"After being there for a year, I left and joined Motherwell on a part-time basis and then my last club as a player was Forfar as I had to stop playing after I had three operations on my knee."

It wasn't the end of Jimmy's football career however as he came back to Dens in 1966 and worked under four different managers as a part-time coach working with the reserves.

"I started in 1966 working part-time under Bobby Ancell, taking the reserves twice a week. I finally left in 1978 after working under several managers and Tommy Gemmell was my last. I did have the chance to join my friend Jim McLean over at Tannadice but I didn't want to as Jim at that time was football twenty-four hours a day and for me at that time, it was a bit too much.

"During the end of my career and my coaching job at Dens, I was working for the production and control department at NCR. That was from 1956 until 1974 and after that I worked at Timex doing the same job

before I retired at the age of 62. I then worked part-time in stock ordering with Fine Home Interiors until I finally gave up in 1989.

"After I retired full-time, I enjoyed playing golf and I have been a member of Downfield Golf Club since 1950 and once had a handicap of four and also like to play bowls as much as I can at Broughty Castle Bowling Club."

"I've got so many great memories from my playing career and was lucky to win three cup winners' medals at Hampden. The Junior Cup winners' medal is special to me as it was my first and the write-ups I got for that game were amazing. Fauldhouse had me training with Celtic at that time and the papers often linked me with them but it was all talk.

"The greatest game I played however has to be the 1952 League Cup semi-final win over Hibs at Tynecastle. That was the semi before the Killie game and we faced up to the Hibs 'Famous Five' who were the reigning League champions at the time and it was a game of total skill between two fantastic teams.

"My disappointments are few and far between but the most annoying thing is that I didn't get an international cap as I got called up a lot but never played. My career however is full of wonderful memories."

Almost sixty years to the day of winning the League Cup Final against Rangers, Jimmy Toner took to the Dens Park pitch once again at half time and deserved the standing ovation he received in recognition of his achievement in winning two major winners' medals with The Dee; something that none of the famous Championship winning team of ten years later achieved.

Honours at Dundee:

Scottish League Cup winners:	1951/52, 1952/53

Appearances, Goals:

League:	51, 14 goals
Scottish Cup:	3, 1 goal
League Cup:	17, 7 goals
Totals:	71, 22 goals

Chapter 15:
The Road and the Miles

A WEEK AFTER the League Cup triumph at Hampden, the trophy was on display at the next match against Raith Rovers at Dens. Around 21,000 jubilant home supporters turned up to glimpse the cup which was 6,000 more than the corresponding league fixture the previous season.

At 2.30pm, the League Cup emerged from the players' tunnel to a huge cheer, carried by four members of the Dundee Cadet Band and it was paraded around the track behind the pipe band of the Cadets. The circumference march of Dens took fifteen minutes to great applause before the trophy was placed on a display table in front of the Main Stand and when the players came out at 2.55pm, they lined up for a group photo with their glittering prize.

The team for the match against Raith was the same eleven that had defeated Rangers and they were joined in the photo by manager George Anderson, trainer Reggie Smith, secretary Bob Crichton, chairman James Gellatly and directors Frank Graham, Andrew Clark and Jack Swadel. Dundee wore the their traditional dark blue shirts for the picture after asking Raith to bring their change kit as it was then traditional for the home side to change. Having worn their white shirts at Hampden, Anderson wanted the posterity photo to have Dundee in dark blue and Raith were only too happy to oblige. (This was to become an iconic photograph of a great Dundee team and later Ian Gellatly in referring to his father in the front row, pointed out that the Dens Park chairman had just four fingers on his left hand, having lost the index finger in a domestic accident)

There was a mood of celebration both on and off the park at Dens that day and this was enhanced by a comfortable 2-0 win thanks to a brace from Bobby Flavell. Incredibly however, by mid-December, Dundee lay second bottom of the league, for that Raith victory was to prove their only win in seven post-Hampden outings. A recurring ankle injury had forced the influential Steel to miss a number of games but the previously reliable defence had lost four goals in successive games against Hibs, East Fife, and Airdrie.

George Anderson therefore turned to his reserves bringing in centre-half George Merchant and inside-right Albert Henderson and with Steel returning, festive wins over Stirling Albion (h) 4-1, Partick (a) 3-1, Third Lanark (a) 2-0, Aberdeen (h) 3-2 and Rangers (a) 2-1 lifted Dundee to sixth. Remarkably the win over the Ibrox men was Dundee's third of the season but with only two points taken from the next three games and their league championship hopes gone, Dundee now looked to the Scottish Cup for further success.

The 1951/52 Scottish Cup was the sixty-seventh staging of Scotland's most prestigious knock-out competition and in the first round Dundee drew Ayr United at home to be played on January 26th. All Scottish League clubs entered in round one alongside four sides from the Scottish Qualifying Cup (North) and four from the Scottish Qualifying Cup (South) and the draw had paired Dundee with a side from the 'B' Division.

Two weeks before Dundee were due to play 'The Honest Men', George Anderson decided to take his squad for a week's break in Troon prior to the league match with Morton in Greenock. A squad of fifteen travelled down to Ayrshire on Friday January 11th the day before the Cappielow game but Gerry Follon and Jack Cowan would miss the trip. Follon was a part-timer at Dens and worked as a secondary school teacher and was unable to take a week off school, while Cowan was an absentee as he had classes at university. Cowan though agreed to play for the reserves at Dens Park against Leith Athletic in a 'C' Division match and his presence helped the 'wee Dark Blues' to a 3-0 win.

Gordon Frew came in a left-back for his only his second game in four months while Johnny Pattillo filled in at right-back for Follon and was outstanding against 'Ton despite the 3-0 defeat.

On Monday, Dundee did some training at Prestwick Airport thanks to a gesture by some U.S. airmen who were stationed there. The Americans had visited Dundee's hotel before the Morton game and offered Dundee the use of their new gym and the Dark Blues gratefully took them up on their offer.

Dundee stayed in a hotel directly across from the Troon Old Course where the previous year's Open Championship had been played and the Dundee players took advantage of this by playing golf every day. On the Tuesday they competed against a team from the West of Scotland Golf Club and on the Wednesday took on Rangers in a four-ball foursomes and beat them for the fourth consecutive year.

On Tuesday Alfie Boyd got the news that his wife had given birth to a son and after the golf left to go to the hospital in Dundee. He already had a six-year-old daughter and when he left the hotel he told reporters that, *"I'm off to see if he's got a good left foot."*

Not everybody was having a great time as by the middle of the week Bobby Flavell was in bed with flu while Bill Brown was anxiously waiting to see if he would be eligible to play against Ayr, who had drawn 0-0 at Tannadice the week before. The keeper was due to report to Padgate on Friday for the start of National Service with the R.A.F. but he was hoping to be released for the cup tie.

Dundee drew 1-1 with Celtic at Dens upon their return from Troon but the build-up to the cup-tie was hampered by heavy snowfall which prevented much training. By Friday, they found the pitch still covered in snow but were able to take part in a full session after the ground staff had piled the snow around the touchline.

Bill Brown got the news he had been waiting for and it was that he had not been released by the R.A.F. to play against Ayr and would not be expected back in the city for at least eight weeks. He would not in fact play for the Dark Blues for another twelve months, missing Dundee's second 'Road to Hampden' and travelled south with George Christie's brother Jim that day, who was also reporting for duty at Padgate.

Bobby Henderson therefore returned in goal as did Follon and Cowan at full-back but the surprise choice was the inclusion of centre-half Andy Irvine at centre-forward to replace the still bedridden Flavell. Irvine's move upfield came after a 'C' Division match against Hibs the previous week, when director Jack Swadel, who accompanied the reserves to Easter Road, suggested Irvine should move up front and did so successfully when he scored. George Anderson therefore decided to repeat the experiment against Ayr and it was a move that paid off when Irvine stunned the 20,000 crowd by scoring twice.

With the snow still piled high around the pitch (described in *The Sporting Post* as a *"Dens ice-cake"*), Pattillo and Steel got the other goals in a comfortable win but it was the performance of Jack Cowan that *The Courier* was raving about on Monday. *"Jack Cowan has never played a finer game for the Dark Blues. His kicking was a treat and he played his 'hook' shots to perfection."*

The second round draw took place at Park Gardens two days later on January 28th with the plum tie being Hearts v Hibs or Raith. The dailies were salivating at the prospect of an Edinburgh derby, but in the event, Rovers stunned the reigning Scottish champions by beating them 4-0 in a second replay at Kirkcaldy.

For Dundee, it was a far less glamorous tie with an away draw against non-league Wigtown & Bladnoch from the Scottish Borders. Wigtown had shocked 'C' Division Montrose in the first round with a 2-1 win at Links Park after an epic journey, leaving Dumfries & Galloway at 3am for the trip to Angus and they now looked forward to hosting the Scottish League Cup holders.

Wigtown & Bladnoch qualified for the Scottish Cup after winning the Qualifying Cup (South), beating Duns 2-0 in both legs of the final and were to have a remarkable season. They also won the South of Scotland Football League and the South of Scotland League Cup and by the time they met Dundee on February 9th they were yet to lose a game that season. They were undefeated since March 1950 but the Dark Blues were still expected to progress comfortably against a non-league side.

The biggest problems for Dundee would be getting there and would the game be on as the winter had claimed Dundee's only match scheduled between the cup ties. The Dark Blues had been due to play Partick Thistle on February 2nd but Dens failed an 8am pitch inspection due to frost and Anderson had concerns about travelling down to Wigtown, if only to find the game off.

Some of the Dundee squad used the afternoon off to go and watch Carnoustie Panmure play Kirkintilloch Rob Roy in the fifth round of the Scottish Junior Cup after Carnoustie borrowed some rubber boots from Dens to combat the frost. Alfie Boyd personally delivered them to the Panmure dressing room and delighted the home team by offering 'some tips'. Rob Roy themselves were wearing rubber boots, bought from Billy Steel's sports shop in Glasgow but they did little good as Carnoustie ran out 4-1 winners.

George Anderson spent the afternoon planning the travel arrangements for Wigtown; a 400-mile, arduous round trip which was going to need some special arrangements and the calling in of some 'wartime' favours.

Wigtown were expecting a bumper crowd and their highest attendance that season had already been 4000, despite only having a population of 1300. The Dundee match was Wigtown's first home cup tie of the season having been drawn away in every match in the Qualifying Cup, South of Scotland and Scottish Cups, but The Dark Blues probably wished they could go back to the tradition of buying 'home rights' from the opposition. They had done just that from Beith in 1910 on the way to winning the trophy but that practice had been scrapped after the First World War and Dundee would just have to be prepared to travel south.

The Partick game had been rearranged for three days before the Wigtown match but again fell foul to frost as one of six matches postponed that evening. A new rule had been introduced that season by the Scottish League that any matches postponed on the Saturday must be rearranged for the following Wednesday but some clubs who were already out of the Scottish Cup wanted to play on the Saturday. The League said no despite the fact that so far every rearranged midweek game had been cancelled and were now farcically rearranged for seven days later with some clubs free to play at the weekend.

Anderson wasn't unhappy that the Thistle game was off as it gave Dundee plenty of time to prepare for the weekend, but with the weather being so poor and the Dens Park track icebound, indoor training was the order of the day. Bobby Flavell showed how well he had got over the flu by doing eighty-four double skips non-stop but failed to break his personal record of 120.

The players also organised a table tennis competition which Bert Henderson won, defeating Basil Wilson in the final.

In the Borders, the news was good with no snow by Thursday, perfect playing conditions and a decent forecast for the weekend, which meant that Dundee could travel south with little chance of the game being called off.

The party left Dundee West Station on the 11.35am train on Friday arriving at Glasgow's Buchanan Street Station at 2.05pm. They then left Glasgow St. Enoch's at 4pm, heading towards

Dumfries where they changed trains (and were met by eighty-year-old Jimmy McKennell, ex-manager of the Queen of the South) and arrived at Newton Stewart at 8.40pm. Dundee stayed in the Galloway Arms Hotel in Newton Stewart, seven miles from Wigtown and on the Friday night were visited at their hotel by Lady Provost of Wigtown, Mrs. Coupland M.B.E. and Provost Barr of Newton Stewart. They were also visited by the officials of Wigtown who brought a football to be signed by the Dundee squad to be raffled off for the benefit of the club and were joined by Dundee chairman James Gellatly who was on his way back from London on business.

The Wigtown Supporters' Club were disappointed that Dundee had bought only forty tickets for the tie claiming to their local press that, *"When we went to Montrose, we took 200 supporters with us."*

The Dundee Supporters' Club was concerned about such a long bus journey in poor weather conditions and George Anderson told their secretary that should their bus be unable to make the journey, then two of their members could travel with the official party by train.

In the event, the Dundee Supporters' Club took its bus, leaving North Lindsay Street in Dundee on Saturday morning at 4am. When they arrived in Wigtown just after lunch, they were greeted by a glorious winter's day and hoped that their heroes could avoid being the victims of a cup upset.

The throb of cup-tie fever had hit the little Galloway county town of Wigtown with a vengeance with Dundee's visit to Trammondford Park, a one-time farm field, the talk of the town. Would Wigtown's record of twenty games won and four drawn since August continue? The locals certainly thought so and all local shops were going to be shut for the duration of the match.

The most excited man in the Wigtown camp was eighty-year-old Pat Hughes, who had not missed a match that season, clocking up over 2,000 miles in doing so. The busiest men in the town were the local barber with all the players and committee wanting to look their best and Wigtown secretary Percy Robb, who was making all the arrangements for the biggest game in the club's sixty-four year history.

He and his committee had a few headaches getting everything ready but team difficulties wasn't one of them as Wigtown only had twelve players on their books. The team would be exactly the same as the one which had won the Qualifying Cup and were top of the South of Scotland League and had reached an impressive four local cup finals. Wigtown president William Graham said to Colin Glen of *The Courier*, *"We are in this game with a definite chance of winning and have a good team of experienced players and can put up a good show."*

There had originally been talk of moving the game away from the tiny ground but Police Chief Hutchison from Stranraer was having none of it saying (with tongue firmly in cheek), *"There is room for 32,000. We could get them all in but whether or not they would all see the game or not is another matter."* The Trammondford Park grandstand only held about 200 but Hutchinson said they would *"Squeeze a few more in."*

No doubt bearing this in mind and determined to give spectators a fair chance to see the game, the match was made all-ticket at a maximum of 6,000 spectators, with prices at 2s, double the usual charge for South of Scotland League matches.

The local railway station was also to be opened for the first time since 1950 for one day only, with football specials being laid on from local stations and people came from a 100-mile radius from the villages scattered around the town.

While the weather didn't put the match in doubt, one event which did was the death of King George VI on Wednesday February 7th. However, on Thursday both the S.F.A. and the F.A. announced that football would be played as normal on the Saturday with all players to wear black arm bands, flags to be flown at half mast and music to be appropriate for the occasion which was exactly the same procedure upon the death of George V in 1936.

By coincidence Wigtown & Bladnoch had only appeared once before in the Scottish Cup in 1936 and on the day they played Albion Rovers there was a minute's silence for the death of George V.

Dundee got a tremendous welcome when they arrived at the ground around 2pm and got a tumultuous cheer from the record 4,500 who were crammed in when they took to the pitch.

Billy Steel was the man they all wanted to see and the Wigtown President William Graham, who owned his own bakery, jokingly offered Steel half-a-dozen of his finest pies in an effort to slow him down. He needn't have bothered however as Billy responded the only way he knew how with an all action display and two goals.

Steel opened the scoring in ten minutes but Wigtown got a chance to live their dream when they equalised on twenty-eight minutes through inside-left Cowan. Trammondford Park went crazy but it was a short-lived dream when Pattillo restored Dundee's lead just two minutes later. Steel got his got his second before George Hill made in 4-1 before half time and Wigtown's dream was well and truly shattered.

Dundee didn't let up in the second half where further scores from Pattillo and Hill and a goal from George Christie gave The Dark Blues a comfortable 7-1 win. It was a day Wigtown & Bladnoch would never forget but it was a banana skin avoided by Dundee who were through to the Monday's third round draw.

Before that however, they had their journey home odyssey for which George Anderson had to make a number of special arrangements with the help of some associates he had met during the war. After the match, a private coach took the Dundee party to Girvan where the London-Glasgow train had made a special stop at 7.45pm just to pick up the Dens Park party. Upon arriving in Glasgow, the late train from Buchanan Street Station was held back until 10.45pm to allow the Dundonians to catch it and when that train terminated in Perth at 12.30am, a special train took the weary group along the River Tay where they finally arrived Dundee West at 1.15am after a marathon eight-hour journey.

Being in the hat for the next round however made the journey worthwhile and hopes were beginning to rise that perhaps Dundee could reach Hampden for the second time that season and complete a cup double.

Chapter 16:
Johnny Pattillo

JOHNNY PATTILLO PLAYED during a golden era at Dens, playing right in the heart of it as a prolific striker who won two winners' medals and two runners-up medals as well as scoring a goal in the 1951 League Cup Final victory to cement his place in Dundee's history.

Born in Aberdeen in 1923, Johnny joined his home town team in 1938 and, like so many players of his generation, had his career interrupted by the Second World War. He joined The Dons one year after their first Scottish Cup Final and left the year before they won the Cup again in 1947 but success was just around the corner for him at Dens. Before he left Pittodrie however he did finish as The Dons' top scorer and won the 1945/46 Southern League Cup against Rangers. The following summer he moved down the east coast to Dundee to join George Anderson's new look Dark Blues for £1,000.

Johnny made his debut for Dundee on the opening day of the season in a 'B' Division match away to East Fife and was on the scoresheet in a 6-2 win. This high scoring Dark Blues' performance was a sign of things to come for the new season as they went on to score five goals or more on sixteen occasions and scored four goals eight times. His debut season saw him score twenty-two times on the way to winning the title and a further four in the Forfarshire Cup where the season ended on a high with a 5-0 home win over Dundee United in the final and Johnny getting one of the goals.

In Dundee's first season back in the big time Pattillo scored fifteen times on the way to a very respectable fourth-placed finish. He improved that rate by two the following year as Dundee also improved their league placing by two, finishing as runners-up in the 'A' Division.

Any hopes that the runners-up spot could be improved on were dashed early the following season with a number of disappointing reverses and incredibly for Pattillo, having scored fifty-five goals in the last three seasons, he now went the whole of 1949/50 season without scoring at all as Dundee finished a disappointing sixth. They had failed to get out of their section in the League Cup and were knocked out in the first round of the Scottish Cup and so clearly something had to change the following year for Johnny and Dundee.

What did change therefore was one of the most audacious signings in Scottish football history as Anderson persuaded superstar Billy Steel to join the Dark Blues for a world record fee of £23,500. Inside-left Steel would join inside-right Pattillo in a new dynamic forward line, alongside former Hearts centre-forward Bobby Flavell who joined shortly afterwards and it wasn't long before the trio shot Dundee to two Hampden cup final appearances in the same season.

The first of those appearances was in the League Cup Final of 1951 and Dundee's 3-2 win over Rangers is one of the best finals the National Stadium has ever seen. Johnny scored in the 5-1 semi-final win over Motherwell at Ibrox but the real glory came for him in the final when he scored the second on sixty-nine minutes. Pattillo ran on to a Flavell through ball and shot high past Brown in the Rangers goal to put the Dark Blues 2-1 ahead.

Dundee returned to Hampden just five months later when they appeared in their second final of the season but there was no joy this time in the Scottish Cup as Motherwell took the trophy back to Lanarkshire with a 4-0 win. Johnny played in the final and all five matches en route, scoring four times, which included a brace against Wigtown in a 7-1 second round away win and the only goal in a 1-0 victory over Berwick at Dens in the next round.

The final against Motherwell proved to be Johnny's penultimate match for Dundee as the following week at Dens against Third Lanark in the final match of the season in the 'A' Division, Johnny made his last appearance in dark blue, unusually at right back!

That summer he moved to his hometown team Aberdeen to take up a coaching role but in February 1953 he was appointed manager of St Johnstone and pulled on their light blue shirt eight times to become one of the first player/managers in Scottish Football history.

Johnny left St Johnstone in 1958 and retired from the game and sadly died aged seventy-nine in August 2002. In his six years at Dens he scored sixty-seven goals, making him twentieth on Dundee's all-time top goalscorers' list, putting him ahead of goalscoring Dens Park luminaries such as Tommy Coyne, Ray Stephen, Iain Ferguson, Nacho Novo, Juan Sara, Alec Stott and George Merchant to name but a few.

He also did something that none of those of other goalscoring legends achieved by winning a major honour and scoring a goal in the final in the process and for that he will always be revered on Sandeman Street.

Honours at Dundee:	
Scottish League Cup winners:	1951/52
Scottish League Championship runners–up:	1948/49
Scottish Cup runners–up:	1952
Scottish League B Division winners:	1946/47

Appearances, Goals:	
League:	123, 43 goals
Scottish Cup:	19, 10 goals
League Cup:	30, 14 goals
Totals:	172, 67 goals

Chapter 17:
Old Friends and New Enemies

ON MONDAY FEBRUARY 11th 1952, the Scottish Cup third round draw was made at 1pm at the S.F.A headquarters and Dundee were delighted when they were given a home draw against either Alloa Athletic or Berwick Rangers who had drawn 0-0 at Recreation Park on Saturday.

It wasn't the only good news received at Dens as popular right-half Tommy Gallacher announced his engagement to Catherine Smith. Catherine was the centre-forward of the Grove Academy F.P. hockey team and the couple were to be married on February 25th, two days after the Scottish Cup third round.

The replay between Berwick and Alloa took place at Shielfield Park on Valentine's Day and the 'C' Division side from just south of the Scottish border shocked their 'B' Division counterparts with a 4-1 win, to set up a date at Dens.

Dundee's preparations for the visit of 'The Wee Gers' wasn't ideal when they lost 2-1 to Motherwell at Dens the week before which gave the Fir Park side a league double over The Dee for the first time since 1933/34. They were, however, taking no chances and on Tuesday 19th had a full scale practice match to try and help get the injured players fit.

Berwick were managed by former Dee (and future manager) Bobby Ancell and had in their ranks the popular Dark Blues' striker Albert Juliussen, who scored goals for fun just after the war. Ancell played for Dundee from 1945 until 1948, winning two 'B' Division championships, while Juliussen also played in those title winning sides, scoring ninety-five goals in just seventy-three appearances. The big Englishman was Dundee's first post-war hero and his seven goals against Dunfermline on March 22nd 1947 is still a club record for most goals in a game (a record shared with Alan Gilzean who scored seven against Queen of the South fifteen years later). The Dundee fans knew that 'Julie' was the man to watch in Black and Gold.

Berwick travelled up to Dundee on Friday night to avoid an early Saturday departure which Ancell, who was suffering from flu, felt might jeopardise their chances. They stayed overnight in a Dundee city centre hotel while two special trains and fourteen buses brought 1,500 Berwick fans to Dens, confident of causing an upset.

Berwick had already faced Dundee 'A' twice that season in the 'C' Division and were undefeated with a 3-3 draw at Dens in September and a 3-2 win at Shielfield in December. They now hoped they could reproduce that form against Dundee's first team.

Dundee United had drawn Aberdeen at home in the same round of the cup and their match with The Dons was allowed to take place at the same time as the Dundee v Berwick tie. Sandeman Street had an extremely busy afternoon with 26,417 at Tannadice and 15,000 at Dens where, despite the loss of 'Pud' Hill with a broken arm, an early Pattillo goal was enough to see Dundee through.

Across the road, United and Aberdeen drew 2-2 and when the quarter-final draw was made two days later it paired the winners of their replay with the Dark Blues at Dens. Within an hour of the draw Dundee announced that it would be all-ticket no matter who the opposition were and the city was excited about the possibility of a Dundee derby in the quarters.

"It's a great incentive for our lads to win at Aberdeen," said United manager Willie McFadyen, while George Anderson said, *"It's a grand draw for us!"*

United were looking for revenge for the first round exit at the hands of The Dark Blues the previous year while Dundee were happy with the chance to play The Dons and get revenge for the marathon 1947 tie which saw Aberdeen score the first ever golden goal. After the tie had been postponed a number of times, the sides were level 1-1 at ninety minutes and again at the end of extra time and with the semi-finals due to be played in a couple of days, the clubs agreed to play a sudden death, next-goal-the-winner scenario.

Aberdeen grabbed the crucial strike in the 129th minute, thereby scoring the first ever 'golden goal' and after defeating Arbroath 2-0 in the semis at Dens, went on to lift the trophy with a 2-1 win over Hibs at Hampden for their first ever success in the Scottish Cup.

It was Dundee who were to get their chance of revenge on March 8th as Aberdeen went on to win the replay 3-2 at Pittodrie and while many were disappointed not to be facing their neighbours, the match against The Dons sparked an unprecedented ticket rush.

The briefs were to go on sale at the end of the next home game at St Mirren on March 1st and supporters started to leave the game at half-time to get into the queue for quarter-final tickets. There were only 12,000 at the 3-0 win over The Buddies but within an hour 26,000 tickets were sold with the main stand completely sold out. The remaining tickets went on sale on Monday at the secretary's office in Reform Street and it was completely besieged as soon as it opened at 10am. By 3.30pm the match was completely sold out with The Dons also selling their allocation of 9,000 tickets.

The match had caught the imagination of both the Dundee and Aberdeen footballing public and with Dens guaranteed a new record sell-out crowd of 41,000, terracing tickets were being exchanged in pubs for as much as 4 or 5s. This was still a time of post-war austerity with the end of rationing still two years away and the price that tickets were being exchanged for *'astonished'* the editorial in *The Courier*.

The match was a special one for George Anderson as he was not only born in the Granite City but was also a town councillor there, had business interests there and had also played for and managed The Dons. Dundee also had Aberdonians Doug Cowie, George Christie and Johnny Pattillo in their side who were all keen to impress against their home town team.

Aberdeen themselves had an old Dens Park acquaintance in their ranks in the guise of manager Davie Halliday who was a Dark Blues goalscoring hero in the Twenties. He was a phenomenal striker who found scoring as natural as breathing and in 1923/24 set a new club record of thirty-eight league goals in one season which still stands today. He joined the Dons as manager in 1937 and when he enlisted in the Second World War, the post was held open for him upon his return. George Anderson filled the void in Halliday's absence but moved to Dens when Halliday thankfully returned and he ushered in a new era of success for Aberdeen, winning the Southern League Cup in 1946 and the Scottish Cup in 1947.

Anderson was keen to emulate the man who held the job he had originally wanted and having won the League Cup himself in October now wanted the Scottish Cup on his C.V. and ironically it was now Halliday who stood in his way of achieving that.

One player due to return to the side was Tommy Gallacher who had missed the last two games since Wigtown as he was on his honeymoon. He returned to training on the Friday but it was cancelled by Anderson due to torrential rain as he didn't want to take any chances and make sure his players were 100% fit.

The pre-match entertainment was provided by the Pipe Band of the 24th Company of the Boys'

Brigade (Dundee St Mary' Parish) who had recently been invited to take part in the Joan of Arc celebrations in Orleans in May. They played from around 2.30pm as the crowds streamed in and by the time kick-off had arrived the atmosphere was at fever pitch.

For the first half an hour of the game Dundee held the upper hand and had two goals chalked off by referee Jack Mowatt for offside. Mowat, who had refereed the League Cup Final in October, was greeted with howls of indignation when he disallowed efforts from winger Gerry Burrell – in for the injured Toner – and Ken Zeising but the referee's supervisor in the stand, Mr J. M. Martin, later stated the Mowat was correct with these decisions.

Also in the stand was the Raith Rovers squad who had knocked the Dark Blues out at the same stage last season. They had been eliminated this year by Hearts in the second round and they witnessed Dundee take the lead when Zeising's drive made it over the line, despite the efforts of Aberdeen left-back Don Emery who fell back into the net in an attempt to stop it.

Aberdeen then came into the game and were unlucky not to equalise when Tommy Pearson hit the bar, but The Dee held on for a 1-0 interval lead. The turning point in the game came five minutes after the restart when Christie and Steel brought off one of their picturesque weaving acts and Billy finished the move by beating Anderson, Thomson and Martin to score.

Steel was on fire and must have impressed the Scottish selectors in the crowd who were there with a view to picking the Scotland side to face England next month and Billy did his chances no harm by getting Dundee's third.

Dundee were terrific, with a superb display of teamwork and finished off a fantastic afternoon when they got their fourth from the penalty spot. Mowatt initially waved away Dundee's appeals when Don Emery fisted Pattillo's shot away but after the winger according to *The Sporting Post*, *'jumped twice the height of himself in outraged protest'* and the linesman had a word, the kick was given and Alfie Boyd made it 4-0.

After the match Aberdeen chairman William Mitchell said, *"We were beaten by the better side. Now I wish Dundee every success and look forward to seeing them bring the Scottish Cup to Tayside,"* while Aberdeen inside-forward Archie Baird said, *"We had a poor, poor game."*

There was some small consolation for the Aberdeen directors when in the Dens Park boardroom they were given the news that Aberdeen reserves had beaten Hearts reserves 4-2 in the semi-final of the Second XI Cup. Director Dick Donald told *The Courier*, *"We have a grand team of youngsters,"* but it was Dundee's day with an impressive result against a decent Dons side.

George Anderson was understandably delighted and now promised to take his players for a week's holiday in the south of England as a reward. After the East Fife league match seven days later, Dundee headed to Southampton for a week of relaxation apart from the Monday night where they took on the Saints at the Dell in a floodlit friendly. A 3-2 win thanks to two goals from Tommy Gallacher and one from Billy Steel just helped put Dundee in holiday mode and the rest of the week was spent with games of golf and day trips, including one to the Isle of Wight on Wednesday.

By then Dundee knew who they would be facing in the semi-final as the draw on Monday March 10th at Hampden paired Dundee with Third Lanark while the other match needed replays to decide it with Hearts or Airdrie drawn against Motherwell or Rangers. The venues were also announced at the draw and Dundee expressed disappointment at the Thirds game being at Easter Road and the other tie at Hampden.

There had been a suggestion beforehand that the pre-war system of having both semis at Hampden a week apart be reintroduced and Dundee felt their tie should have been at Hampden as they were definitely playing a side from Glasgow. Anderson described the decision as *"puzzling"* and suggested to *The Courier* that the S.F.A must be banking on Rangers getting through their replay with Motherwell to already announce that semi at Hampden. He said that semi-final attendances in

Edinburgh for matches that do not include either capital side are traditionally low and pointed out that only 30,000 turned up for the Dundee v Clyde Scottish Cup semi in 1949. *"The Edinburgh football public"* said Dundee's managing-director, *"do not normally turn up for games involving neutral teams."*

In the event Motherwell defeated Rangers 2-1 at Fir Park in their replay and Hearts defeated Airdrie 6-4 which meant that one semi-final including one Edinburgh team and no Glasgow side would be at Hampden and the other semi with one Glasgow side and no Edinburgh club would be at Easter Road!

If Dundee were unhappy with the venue, they were delighted at drawing Third Lanark with *The Courier* saying, *'Dundee's chances of making the Final are rosy.'* George Anderson said he was, *"Delighted with the news. It's a great draw,"* and captain Alfie Boyd showed confidence by stating, *"We'll have to watch our step but we can beat Thirds."*

Another puzzling decision announced at the draw was that any replays would not be played the following Wednesday but on Monday April 7th because of the Scotland v England game at Hampden on April 5th. The S.F.A. said that the annual England game was too big a match to risk injuries to key players three days beforehand but the clubs were perplexed with the decision to have the replays on a Monday.

Once the quarter-final replays were held, all four semi-finalists asked the S.F.A. to reconsider the venues and swap them over to save thousands unnecessarily travelling between Edinburgh and Glasgow but on Tuesday March 18th the S.F.A. said no. They declared this when they announced the referees for the semis and for the Dundee v Thirds game and the man in charge was to be the experienced Charlie Faultless.

Once again, like for the League Cup semi and final, they was a rush on coach hire in Dundee with buses being imported in from Kirriemuir and Arbroath.

Tickets for the Thirds game would only be required for the stand with the terracing being pay at the gate and prices were set at 10s 6d, 7s 6d and 5s. Dundee were again unhappy as they received only 12½% of the stand, as did Third Lanark and the hosts Hibernian with the S.F.A. taking the rest and George Anderson announced that there would therefore be no public sale of tickets.

The S.F.A. had to backtrack on this when they couldn't sell their tickets and went back to Dundee and offered them extra. This allowed the Dark Blues to put some briefs on public sale and they were quickly snapped up with an estimated 15,000 travelling through to Easter Road.

For Third Lanark this was their first time past the third round since the war and they were going into the semi in confident mood with a recent a good run in the league. Manager Alex Ritchie took his side for a week's break to the south of Scotland and he was hopeful that they could reach their first final since 1936.

Johnny Pattillo was a doubt for the game with an ankle injury but the Dark Blues' main concern was Billy Steel, whose own ankle injury had forced the S.F.A. to drop him for the Scotland v England game. He failed to turn up at Dens for treatment on Wednesday three days before, promising to turn up on Thursday, and the chances of Dundee's superstar being ready looked slim.

Steel was magnanimous when dropped by Scotland and phoned his replacement Ian McMillan of Airdrieonians to congratulate him. He said that Dundee knew he had been playing with a handicap but thankfully he passed a fitness test on Friday, along with Bobby Flavell and Johnny Pattillo.

Steel took to the Easter Road pitch on March 29th with his leg heavily strapped and there to watch him and his team mates was Bill Brown who was on leave to watch the match before reporting to a new unit in Wiltshire on Monday.

From the kick-off there was little between the sides but it was Dundee, wearing their change white kit, who made the vital breakthrough on twenty-seven minutes thanks to a piece of brilliance from Steel. When a cross came into from George Christie, Steel had the tenacity to dummy it which allowed Gerry Burrell to fire it home from six yards.

Right-winger Burrell was only in the side because of injuries to both Jimmy Toner and George Hill and would play only twelve times that season (and only thirty-nine Dundee games in total) but he had written his place in Dark Blue history with a priceless goal.

Thirds hit back with an onslaught on Dundee's goal but three minutes before half-time Billy Steel scored a goal described by *The Sporting Post* as *'a goal in a thousand.'* Their description was as follows: *"On forty-two minutes came a marvellous goal. Henderson threw the ball to Cowan who slipped it to Gallacher. Tommy sent it to Steel. A pass to Steel. Back to Flavell. Steel received possession again fifteen yards out. He hopped twice on his right foot following the ball and then with his left foot flashed in an unsaveable shot."*

One minute, thirty-five seconds of Pathé News footage survives on YouTube and on fifty-nine seconds you can just about see Billy's thing of beauty from a behind the goal camera. It was moments like this that justified the huge outlay Dundee had splashed on the mercurial Steel.

At the break Bobby Flavell had to get an injection from Dundee's medic Dr. Nelson on the thigh strain which had made him a pre-match doubt and this kept the centre going for the second period, if not at full speed, at least effectively.

Billy Steel managed the full ninety minutes despite feel a few twinges of pain on his ankle but at the end declared he felt fine and *"very happy."* This was because there was no more scoring in the second half and Dundee were through to their third Scottish Cup Final with a 2-0 win. Third Lanark had put everything they had into the second half but became anxious and nervy as the game wore on and Dundee's defence had all the answers to their moves.

The victory was Dundee's first at Easter Road since the war and with the other semi between Motherwell and Hearts being drawn 1-1, George Anderson stated, *"Either team in the Final will suit us."*

Telegrams from all over the country arrived to congratulate Dundee, including one from Southampton F.C. whom the Dark Blues had recently met in a friendly. George Anderson's staff at his confectionery business in Aberdeen sent one as did Jock Shaw of Rangers which said, *"All the best. I think it is your turn"* while Dundee Lord Provost Fenton wired, *"All my good wishes on a grand victory today."*

It was a historic day for The Dee, through to their second cup final that season; the only time in their history they achieved such a feat. The Scottish Cup was the cup of dreams for many and Dundee were now dreaming of winning it for the first time in a generation.

Chapter 18:
Bobby Flavell

TO SCORE A goal in a winning cup final for Dundee is pretty special but to do it twice is incredible and only one man has achieved this tremendous feat. When Dundee became the first side to win back to back League Cups in 1951 and 1952, Bobby Flavell wrote himself into the Dark Blue history books by scoring in both victorious finals.

Robert Flavell was an exceptional forward who was born in Annathill in North Lanarkshire on September 1st 1921 and he joined the senior game by signing for Airdrieonians in 1940. He had to wait until the 1946/47 season to make a league appearance, due to the Second World War and during the conflict, Flavell had made guest appearances for both Arsenal and Spurs. When the Scottish Football League resumed in 1946, Flavell scored over a goal per game for Airdrie and won two full caps for Scotland, which convinced Hearts to pay £10,000 to acquire his services.

He again scored frequently at Tynecastle, but he became a football outcast in 1950 by signing for Millonarios of the breakaway Colombian league. Bankrolled by cattle barons, this league was unrecognised by F.I.F.A. and proved to be a controversial career advancement plan for a determined group of British players such as Stoke's centre-half Neil Franklin, Manchester United's Charlie Mitten and Bobby Flavell.

Money was the main draw for top European players and Flavell played alongside Alfredo Di Stefano for the Bogota-based Millonarios and maintained a friendship with the great man, meeting up again at the Champions League Final in Glasgow in 2000. The side became renowned for its artistry and was nicknamed the 'Ballet Azul' (Blue Ballet) and after eighteen months in South America, Bobby returned to Scotland where he signed for Dundee.

He officially joined the Dark Blues from Hearts as the Tynecastle side still held his registration and he made his competitive debut on the first day of the 1951/52 season away to St. Mirren in the League Cup where he scored in a 2-2 draw.

That match in Paisley was the first on the 'Road to Hampden' as Dundee went all the way to the final. Flavell had quickly struck up a potent partnership with Billy Steel and in the semi-final against Motherwell at Ibrox, he scored a hat-trick in an impressive 5-1 win to see The Dark Blues through to the Hampden showpiece.

At half-time in the final Dundee went in 1-0 down but two minutes after the restart, they were back on level terms when the ever alert Flavell fired home a cross from George Christie, despite the best efforts of Rangers keeper Bobby Brown and the Dark Blues went on to lift the cup with a memorable 3-2 win.

Twelve months later, Dundee were back at Hampden for a third time, having lost the Scottish Cup Final to Motherwell in April and this time they faced 'B' Division Kilmarnock on October 25th 1953 as Dundee tried to successfully defend their League Cup.

Flavell had scored nine goals en route to Hampden, including a hat-trick against old club Airdrie in a sectional tie and Dundee's second in the semi-final win against league champions Hibs where Billy

Steel got the first, but now he would be the sole hero in the final.

With just ten minutes left, Dundee made the breakthrough after being under the cosh for most of the game when Jimmy Toner sent the perfect pass to Flavell and the wee centre shot low past Niven into the Ayrshire side's goal. Six minutes later, Dundee made certain when a Bobby Henderson long punt reached the Killie penalty area and, as centre-half Thyne hesitated, Flavell raced in to thump the bouncing ball into the corner of the net.

'*Hampden Smash-And-Grab by Flavell*', proclaimed the headline in *The Courier* on the Monday but Dundee didn't care as they became the first side to retain the Scottish League Cup.

At the end of the season, Flavell finished as the Dark Blues' top scorer for the second season in a row with twenty-five goals, wearing the number nine shirt with which he became synonymous.

After enjoying a two month summer tour of South Africa, in which Bobby scored fifteen goals in Dundee's seventeen-match visit, he started the new season in the same goalscoring form by grabbing four in a 6-1 League Cup win over Stirling Albion in the first game.

However, after scoring seven goals in eighteen starts by Christmas, the ageing Flavell found himself out of the team as George Merchant moved from centre-half to centre-forward and started scoring goals. He therefore moved to Kilmarnock for two years before transferring to St. Mirren where he would later become manager and knock Dundee out of the Scottish Cup in their Championship season.

Flavell however will be remembered for more glorious cup exploits with Dundee and his sixteen goals in the two League Cup campaigns in the early Fifties did as much as anything to help Dundee win back to back trophies for the only time in the club's history.

Honours at Dundee:	
Scottish League Cup winners:	1951/52, 1952/53
Scottish Cup runners-up:	1952
Appearances, Goals:	
League:	68, 32 goals
Scottish Cup:	6
League Cup:	24, 21 goals
Totals:	98, 53 goals

Chapter 19:
Well Beaten

THREE DAYS AFTER reaching the Scottish Cup Final, George Anderson became the first manager to announce the list of players who would be re-signing for the following season. At this time clubs retained the registrations of the players even if they were out of contract and he announced on April 1st the first ten players who had already signed new deals for the 1952/53 season. These players were:

Backs – Gerry Follon, Alan Massie

Half-Backs – Alfie Boyd, Doug Cowie, George Merchant, Andy Irvine, Bob Henderson, Danny Malloy

Forwards – Johnny Pattillo, George Christie.

Anderson promised others would follow but his immediate concern was the home match with Morton on April 2nd. There were five changes from the side which had beaten Third Lanark in the semi-final as in came Irvine, Merchant, Ziesing, Ewen and Hill to replace Gallacher, Cowie, Flavell, Steel and Christie. Cowie had injured a shoulder against Thirds, Steel and Flavell were under treatment for leg injuries while Christie was rested and those who came in struggled to earn a 2-2 draw with a Greenock side who would be relegated at the end of the season. Only 7,500 turned up for the Wednesday 5pm kick-off, the lowest crowd at Dens since a 'B' Division match against Dumbarton in April 1947.

Dundee had already received a lot of interest in Cup Final tickets and the main office at Dens had a steady stream of enquiries before, during and after the Morton game. The following day, George Anderson told *The Courier* that there would be an announcement about Hampden tickets after the semi-final replay between Motherwell and Hearts which was due to take place on Monday and asked fans to stop calling at Dens until arrangements were made public.

On Friday, Dundee Lord Provost Fenton told *The Evening Telegraph* that there would be a civic reception for The Dark Blues should they win the cup. This came after Mr. J. C. Adamson raised it as a matter of urgency at the town council meeting on Thursday night as he wanted the city to recognise the achievements of the club. At the meeting Adamson also suggested that the council should financially reward the players if they won, recalling that *"When Bob Crumley's boys brought the Scottish Cup to Dundee in 1910 they each received £15 from the city and following public subscription were presented with another £30."*

The Lord Provost replied that he didn't want to embarrass the Dens Park club and any such discussion should wait until after the final and when pressed by Adamson about whether there would be a dinner win or lose, Fenton told the Councillor, *"Don't let us say as you will bring bad luck to them!"*

Friday also saw the announcement of the Scottish Cup Final referee by the S.F.A. and it was to be the same man who officiated at the League Cup Final in October, Mr Jack Mowat, who would take charge of his third final in a row. The linesmen were also announced as Mr J. Brownlie from

Bishopbriggs and Mr. D. Noble from Forfar, who was a minister in the Angus town and joined the S.F.A. list of referees in 1948.

Noble was also a linesman for the Scottish Cup semi-final replay between Heart of Midlothian and Motherwell at Hampden Park on Monday April 7th and with a 1-1 draw after extra-time, the sides would have to do it all again forty-eight hours later. The original match had seen long periods where the crowd became disinterested but the replay was a thriller and was packed with incident in front of 80,209 fans.

The Dark Blues were well represented at the replay as George Anderson was accompanied by Reggie Smith, Andy Irvine, Alfie Boyd, Billy Steel, George Hill, Doug Cowie, Gerry Burrell and Bobby Henderson. Anderson met with S.F.A. officials to discuss cup final ticketing arrangements and was told Dundee would get their allocation on Thursday. He was told that admission to the North and South Stands would be by ticket, as would the South Enclosure while the rest of the ground would be by pay-at-the-gate.

There was no one from Dens at the second replay however as Dundee had a match against Hibs at Easter Road and the Hibees had to beat The Dark Blues to win the Scottish League Championship for the second year in a row. Dundee shocked their hosts on four minutes when they took the lead thanks to George Christie, who had been restored to the side, but two goals in the last nine minutes of the half from Willie Ormond put Hibernian's Championship destiny firmly in their hands. Bobby Combe sealed the 'A' Division title ten minutes after the interval when he made it 3-1 and all three goals were set up by Gordon Smith, who would win the League Flag with Dundee ten years later.

With their superior goal average, Hibs now couldn't be caught and were Champions of Scotland. They would eventually win the league by four points to give them their third title in five years but their triumph wasn't the news that made the sports headlines the next morning. Most of the papers' main story was the result of the Scottish Cup semi-final replay the same night which showed the regard the Scottish Cup was held in, in comparison to the League Championship.

It was won by Motherwell who beat Hearts by three goals to one to set up a date with Dundee and give them the chance to make up for their final defeat to Celtic twelve months previously. With the 'Well winning the 1950/51 League Cup and reaching the Scottish Cup the same season, they had now reached three major finals out of four while their opponents Dundee had copied their achievement of reaching both major finals in the same season.

The three semi-final matches between Motherwell and Hearts had given George Anderson plenty of chances to put the Lanarkshire side under the microscope and *The Daily Record* said that, *"Motherwell had beaten Hearts by teamwork rather than individualism"* and that the Final with Dundee *"was too close to call."*

Dundee had also profited from the Steelmen-Jam Tarts epic as the semi-final gate receipts were divided equally between the four participants. An incredible 238,214 had watched the three ties at Hampden and added to the 23,615 at Easter Road, the Dark Blues would get a quarter of the substantial cash generated.

Arrangements could now be made for the big day on April 19th and British Rail announced that ten football specials would be making the trip from Dundee to Glasgow for a return fare of 11s 6d. The trains would leave between 8.40am and 11.10am with the last two going direct to King's Park, the nearest station to Hampden, while six football specials would travel from Motherwell.

Dundee's next match at home to Partick Thistle on April 12th was their last match before the cup final which meant George Anderson had plenty to think about in his team selection. Bobby Flavell was rested as his groin injury was troubling him after the Hibs game and Jimmy Fraser came in to replace him for his first game since he broke his leg in a friendly against Blairgowrie the previous year. Anderson hoped that a week's rest would see his sixteen-goal hit man fit for Hampden while

Tommy Gallacher missed out after twisting a knee and jarring an ankle coaching schoolboys during the week.

In front of 16,000 The Dark Blues' minds were perhaps on seven days time as they went down limply by two goals to nil, meaning that they had failed to win a game since the semi-final victory over Third Lanark.

Twenty-four hours later the majority of the squad were at Panmure Church in Monifieth for the christening of Alfie Boyd's infant son Graeme Ean and on Monday the cup final build-up got properly underway both on and off the park.

The tickets went on sale at 10am at Dens and queues started to form at 5.30am. By the time the office had opened the queue was right the way along Sandeman Street, down Provost Road and Dens Road the length of the ground. Dundee were disappointed with their allocation, having only been given 1850 tickets with only 1600 for the South Stand and 250 for the South Enclosure. There were orders already at Dens for ten times that from all over Scotland and England but after a Sunday night meeting of the directors, the club decided to put their briefs on public sale.

At the head of the queue was John Fullerton, son of the secretary of the Dundee Supporters' Club and there were plenty of schoolboys keeping places in the queue for adults and getting tips of between 2s and 3s for their help.

Tickets were gone in less than an hour and one of the last to be sold at 7s 6d was touted to someone further down the queue for 3s more when the shutters went down at the office. Thousands were left disappointed and would now have to take their chances at the cash turnstiles on Saturday but one man whose postal application was accepted was George Comrie.

Comrie, who lived in Billy Steel's birthplace of Denny had been Dundee's left-half in their 1910 Scottish Cup victory over Clyde and had sent in a request by letter and Anderson made sure that the Dundee cup winner got a ticket courtesy of the club.

One man who queued and didn't get a ticket was Willie Gibson who was an outside-left with Dundee fifty years before and won a Dewar Shield medal with The Dark Blues. Gibson was sitting disconsolately on a car bonnet when he was spotted by *Courier* reporter Colin Glen who, after speaking to Willie, went into Dens to tell George Anderson. The managing-director then came out into Sandeman Street and gave him a complimentary ticket and Gibson duly gave 'Toffee Dod' a hug and declared himself the *"happiest man in Dundee."*

Anderson also invited a group of relatives from Hayden Bridge, the Northumbria village where he grew up to attend the final and they were to be joined by the local junior team and committee on their day out to Glasgow. Cup final fever hit the village and the forty-seat bus they booked wasn't big enough, meaning five of the team had to make the trip by taxi and Anderson arranged that they would be entertained to lunch and tea and meet the Dundee players before the match.

On the Wednesday Johnny Pattillo, who had been offered a new deal at Dens, was offered the post of trainer-coach at his former club Aberdeen to replace the retiring Bob McDermid. Johnny accepted the job with his hometown team but would be seeing the season out with Dundee, desperate to go out on a high at Hampden.

The Dundee squad had a full training session on Wednesday with Flavell doing a double session in the morning and afternoon in an effort get fit for Saturday. He was full of running and was kicking the ball without any effect on his groin muscles and Anderson was hopeful he'd make the final.

Tommy Gallacher was exempted from training as his right ankle was still swollen and Reggie Smith sent him to hospital for an x-ray before going home himself, unwell with flu.

George Anderson told the players that a party of fourteen were to travel to Hampden and those lucky enough were Henderson, Follon, Cowan, Gallacher, Cowie, Boyd, Irvine, Ziesing, Burrell, Hill, Pattillo, Flavell, Steel and Christie. They were to leave on Friday, following the same arrangements as for the League Cup Final in October with the wives and girlfriends travelling through on Saturday morning on the 9.40am train before having lunch with their partners at the team's hotel.

Motherwell manager George Stevenson announced his team on the Tuesday and had little desire to change things with only one defeat in the last twenty. They had gone on a bad run after losing 5-1 to Dundee in the League Cup semi but their recent run started on December 29th after they had signed Charlie Cox and Tommy Sloan from Hearts.

The majority of the press thought that the game was too close to call between the winners of the 1950 and the 1951 League Cups but the Steelmen were definitely the side in form. Dundee had failed to win any of their last five league games and had lost twice 2-1 to Motherwell in the 'A' Division but their emphatic victory at Ibrox in October gave Dundee plenty of hope. There also wasn't much to choose between the sides in the league table with Dundee finishing eighth, one place and three points behind the Fir Park side and both were confident they could bring the cup home.

One man who wasn't making the trip to Hampden was Motherwell secretary John 'Sailor' Hunter who had stopped making trips to away games three years before. He was a legend at both clubs after scoring the winner for Dundee in the 1910 Scottish Cup Final and managed Motherwell to the Scottish League Championship in 1932, but he couldn't be persuaded to take in the match at the National Stadium.

On Friday the Dundee Traffic Police issued notice for bus drivers and motorists travelling to Hampden. It said: *"Owing to closure of the road bridge at Castlecary, all heavy traffic - such as buses and lorries – bound for Glasgow will be routed by Dennyloanhead, via Kilsyth. Cars will be permitted to use the bridge route which will be especially open for cup final traffic."*

The Dundee party were travelling by train and left Juteopolis at 3pm, waved off by about 200 well wishers. They seemed in good mood with George Anderson telling the attending press that, *"Reggie Smith, Rueben Bennett and myself have done everything we can for the boys. Now it is up to them and we feel they will not fail us on the field."*

Captain Alfie Boyd was also interviewed on the platform and sounding confident said, *"We are out to play for our own reputations and for the honour of our club and city."*

They arrived at their hotel just after 5pm and, after having a light supper, attended the Empire Theatre in Glasgow. Before they left they were visited at their hotel by the U.S. Navy Commander High and his wife who had entertained the Dark Blues on their trip to Istanbul the previous summer and George Anderson invited them to join the official party at Hampden on Saturday.

Billy Steel met his team mates at the hotel after working in his sports shop during the day and sales had been brisk with his specially made Dundee cup final rosettes.

Dundee arrived at Hampden Park on Saturday afternoon at 2pm and there to greet them was Dundee Lord Provost Fenton who was there as a guest of the S.F.A. Mr. Fenton had been due to attend a luncheon of the Scottish Commercial Travellers' Association of which he was president but he sent his apologies saying, *"Sometimes in life there are things just too important to miss."*

A huge crowd was descending upon Mount Florida and the gates were closed right on kick off with an astonishing 136,274 inside. Over 4,000 fans were locked outside, including 1,000 from Dundee whose special train had arrived late and a large number who had travelled by bus and had been delayed by the Kilsyth detour. Six arrests were made in the ensuing scenes, all from Dundee!

The Dundee v Motherwell crowd is a Scottish Cup record for two provincial sides with only the 1937 Final between Celtic and Aberdeen (147,365) attracting a bigger attendance. It is the fourth highest attendance in the history of Hampden Park (and Scottish football) and the biggest crowd of any match involving Dundee Football Club by some margin.

When the players came out the tunnel there was a deafening roar and Dundee took to the field in a brand new white away kit. Motherwell were wearing their traditional claret and amber shirts but

Anderson wanted Dundee to wear white after their success in that colour in the League Cup Final. It was a brand new kit with blue shorts, blue socks with two white hoops and white long sleeved shirt with a blue collar and cuffs.

Significantly, the shirt had a club badge on it and it was the first ever shirt and therefore the first ever match in which Dundee wore a badge. The design was the letters D, F, and C sloping from right to left in blue on a white shield with blue bordering and it was used by Dundee on both home and away kits for the next three years.

The teams lined up as follows (with positions in brackets):

Dundee: Bobby Henderson (gk), Gerry Follon (rb), Jack Cowan (lb), Tommy Gallacher (rh), Doug Cowie (ch), Alfie Boyd (lh) capt., George Hill (rw), Johnny Pattillo (ir), Bobby Flavell (cf), Billy Steel(il), George Christie (lw).

Motherwell: John Johnson (gk), Willie Kilmarnock (rb) capt., Archie Shaw (lb), Charlie Cox(rh), Andy Paton (ch), Willie Redpath (lh), Tommy Sloan (rw), Wilson Humphries (ir), Archie Kelly (cf), Jimmy Watson (il), Johnny Aitkenhead (lw).

By coincidence both sides fielded eight players who had won the League Cup in the last two seasons and now they were determined to add a Scottish Cup winners' medal to their collections.

Dundee started the brightest and straight from kick off went streaming down the park and split the Motherwell defence wide open. From only ten yards out however and with just the keeper to beat, Johnny Pattillo mishit his shot which went past the post in an almighty let off for the Fir Park side.

Wind assisted Dundee continued to dominant the first half and were desperately unlucky not to be ahead. Three times 'Well skipper Willie Kilmarnock kicked the ball off the line and weeks later, when he met Tommy Gallacher at Rosemount Golf Club in Blairgowrie, Willie sheepishly admitted that at least two had been over the line. Dundee protested furiously after the third clearance but referee Mowat waved played on and at half time, the sides went into the dressing rooms level.

Billy Steel had started brightly and looked in match winning form but, shadowed by Charlie Cox, he took some very heavy tackles and gradually faded from the game.

Motherwell fans were in no doubt who the Dark Blues' danger man was as a section of their support carried a banner with the slogan, *'Steel! We have handled it all our life. No danger'.* (A reference to the fact that Motherwell was the steel production capital of Scotland in Nineteenth and Twentieth Centuries and often nicknamed Steelopolis in the same way Dundee was renowned for jute production amongst other things and was nicknamed Juteopolis)

Everywhere Steel went, right-half Cox went and keeping the 'Pocket Dynamo' quiet was seen as the key to any potential Motherwell victory. When Cox needed reinforcements, Paton and Humphries were on the job and Steel often had to beat three men before he could get a pass in.

Motherwell slowly gained in confidence and when George Christie missed a great chance just after the break, the writing was on the wall for Dundee. The turning point came eleven minutes into the second half when Motherwell got a 'lucky break' when an Alfie Boyd pass meant for Gallacher swerved in the opposite direction to the feet of Humphries. He pounced and carried the ball forward before slipping it to Watson, who easily put the ball past Henderson to give Motherwell the lead.

Dundee reeled under this blow but sixty seconds later it got worse when Motherwell made it two. The Steelmen got another 'lucky break' when left-half Willie Redpath had a happy-go-lucky shot at the Dundee goal and it was going well wide before it struck Alf Boyd's knee and sailed into the goal away from Henderson.

Dundee's main mistake from there on in was trying to play an offside trap and Motherwell were springing it with alarming regularity as the match wore on and scored another lightning double to make it 4-0 before the end. On both occasions the players were played in from the halfway line as the Dundee defensive line pushed up. Firstly, Kelly held the ball up until he could play Wilson Humphries in and then six minutes before the end, Humphries returned the compliment for Kelly to run in and score.

There were never four goals in it but the final score was 4-0 to the Lanarkshire side and the Scottish Cup was on its way to Fir Park for the first time in its history. Motherwell's plan to mark Steel out of the game had paid off and they had also shown more speed and flair for which Dundee's offside ploy was unable to cope. They had written themselves into Fir Park folklore and after the match dedicated their win to John Hunter, saying that they had done it for him.

Henderson and Gallacher had performed well for Dundee but the gamble of playing Flavell - recently plagued with thigh and groin injuries - rather than Ken Ziesing had failed, with only Steel showing anything up front.

A disconsolate Dundee returned home by train on Saturday evening and were welcomed by a few hundred well wishers, but it was a sombre mood at Dundee West Station unlike the welcome of six months before. It been a bitterly disappointing day for Dundee and never have they had a better chance to win the Scottish Cup in their four finals since their solitary 1910 victory.

The players didn't have long to mull over the defeat however as they were in action just forty-eight hours later and would play in three games in the next six days. On Monday afternoon they travelled north to play Aberdeen in the Mitchell Cup and in front of 9,000 slow handclapping Dons, won 2-1 thanks to two goals from Bobby Flavell.

The Mitchell Cup was a trophy presented by Aberdeen chairman William Mitchell in September 1945 to foster a healthy rivalry between Aberdeen and Dundee and having won the first leg 3-0 at Dens a week earlier, Dundee lifted the cup with a 5-1 aggregate win. Also known as the Inter-City Cup, it was the second time Dundee had won it outright (two of the first three competitions were shared) and Dundee would be victorious again the following season - just before the League Cup Final - with a 1-1 draw at Pittodrie and a 2-0 win at Dens. The trophy resides in Aberdeen's boardroom today.

Eight of the side who played at Hampden turned out at Pittodrie, while the other three played in the 'C' Division match against Stirling Albion at Dens the same night and the depth of Dundee's squad was again emphasised again two days later. While the first team were playing in Morton's Willie Westwater's testimonial match at Cappielow, the reserves were facing Hibs 'A' in the 'C' Division and the 4-0 victory clinched the third tier league title for The Dee.

In Greenock, Dundee ran out 7-1 winners with Billy Steel absolutely sensational and involved in all seven goals. Jimmy Fraser scored four and South African Basil Wilson got one but it was Steel against his former club who stole the show, scoring two of the goals himself.

On Saturday Dundee played their last game of the season against Third Lanark at Dens and shook off some of the ghosts of Hampden with an emphatic 6-0 over the Glasgow side. The Scottish Cup Final wasn't the traditional end of season match it is nowadays and the league campaign still had to be completed seven days later. After a busy week Dundee still managed to put on a masterly display and won thanks to goals from Christie, Henderson (2) and a hat-trick from Flavell.

At the end of the match there was a special cheer for Johnny Pattillo who had played his last game for Dundee before taking up his coaching post at Pittodrie and he was carried off shoulder high by Cowie and Boyd. After six successful years at Dens, he had scored sixty-seven goals in 172 appearances and headed back to the Granite City with a 'B' Division winners' medal and a Scottish League Cup winners' medal in his pocket.

Johnny got both his medals after the win over Third Lanark when the players and officials were invited into the Dens Park boardroom by chairman James Gellatly to be presented with their League Cup winners' medals. The Scottish League didn't present winners' medals until 1957 and so Dundee were granted permission to issue their own to players and backroom staff and they were also

Here We Go: Alfie Boyd leads his team out for the 1951 League Cup Final against Rangers.

In Safe Hands: Bill Brown safely gathers ahead of future
Dundee manager Willie Thornton in the 1951 League Cup Final

Go, Johnny Go: Johnny Pattillo is congratulated by team mates after putting Dundee 2-1 ahead in the 1951 League Cup Final

Super Tommy: Tommy Gallacher won the League Cup with Dundee in 1951 and was inducted into the club's Hall of Fame in 2011

Record Breaker: Dundee paid a world record fee for the magical Billy Steel

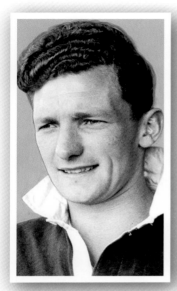

Hit the Right Tone: Jimmy Toner won two League Cups with Dundee and his late positional switch was key to winning the 1952 Final

Captain Fantastic: Alfie Boyd lifts the League Cup aloft after scoring a last minute winner in the 1951 Final against Rangers

Iconic: Dundee show off the League Cup at Dens the week after the 1951 Final

Theatre of Dreams: The Beautiful Dens Park as it looked in 1952

Record Crowd: An astonishing 136,900 fans watch Motherwell keeper John Johnston dive at the feet of Johnny Pattillo in the 1952 Scottish Cup Final

Tumbledown: Motherwell's Archie Kelly appeals for a penalty in the Scottish Cup Final as Johnny Aitkenhead takes a tumble in the Dundee box watched by Dark Blues' Jack Cowan, Doug Cowie, Bobby Henderson and Gerry Follon

Disappointment: Jack Cowan can't prevent Wilson Humphries scoring Motherwell's third in the 1952 Scottish Cup Final

*The Management: Reggie Smith, George Anderson and Reuben Bennett led
Dundee to three Hampden finals within twelve months*

*Tynecastle Heroes: Match programme for
the 1952 League Cup semi-final with
Hibernian at Tynecastle*

*Goalkeeping Great: Bobby Henderson is the
only keeper in the history of Dundee to have
played in two major cup finals*

Hampden Hero: Bobby Flavell's two goals against Kilmarnock won the 1952 League Cup for Dundee

Touch of an Angel: Doug Cowie has the most appearances (446) of any player in the Dark Blues history

Glittering Prize: Alfie Boyd shows off the League Cup to fans at Buchanan Street train station after the 1952 League Cup Final

CABANAS

TRADE MARK

THE SPORTSMAN'S CHOICE

WORN AND ENDORSED BY THE WORLD RENOWNED DUNDEE FOOTBALL TEAM THROUGHOUT THEIR S.A. TOUR

TOP ROW: J. Stewart, Hal Stewart, A. Henderson, J. Stewart, K. Ziesing, D. Cowie, G. Frew, R. Turnbull, J. Cowan, A. Creighton (Director).
CENTRE ROW: M. Shackleton (S.A. Manager), Reg Smith (Trainer), A. Boyd (Captain), T. Gallacher, R. Henderson, N. Stein (Director, Trouser House), G. Anderson (Hon. Manager), J. Irvine, D. Easson, M. Welch (S.T.F.A.).
BOTTOM ROW: T. Daniels (S.T.F.A.), G. Hill, R. Walker, W. Steele, R. Flavell, G. Christie.

TYPOART

World Renowned Dundee: The Dundee players trade on their fame advertising Cabana sports wear during their South African tour

Tartan Troops: Billy Steel wearing the Anderson tartan strip during the 1953 tour of South Africa

Celebration: 1952 League Cup Final match programme and signed menu from the celebration dinner at the Royal British Hotel

presented with tankards for taking part in the St. Mungo's Cup the previous summer.

The players who were part of the 1946/47 'B' Division Championship team five years earlier were also presented with a winners' medal and Mr. Gellatly explained that it had taken so long to present them because there had been a difficulty getting the gold for them! Those who received them were Reggie Smith, Reuben Bennet (who were players then), Gerry Follon, George Hill, Alfie Boyd, Ernie Ewen, Doug Cowie and Johnny Pattillo whom the chairman thanked by saying he knew of no more loyal servant.

George Anderson also paid tribute to Pattillo rating him as one of his most successful deals having only cost £1,000 and said he was *"losing a real pal."* He paid tribute as well to the loyalty of the players and said, *"I would like to thank you all for everything you have done to make this an outstanding season, one of the greatest in the club's history."*

He was right; it was one of the greatest seasons in the club's history with the first silverware won in forty-one years with a second major cup final appearance to boot. The club had also won the Scottish League 'C' Division and the League Cup victory was only Dundee's second major trophy in their fifty-eight year history. The team of Brown, Follon, Cowan, Gallacher, Cowie, Boyd, Toner, Pattillo, Flavell, Steel, Christie had written themselves into Dens Park folklore.

They beat Rangers three times in a season for the first time in their history as well as securing a win and a draw with Celtic and record crowds had turned up to watch Dundee both home and away. They had well and truly arrived as one of the top sides in the country and Dundee had finally rid themselves of the 'nearly men' tag that had plagued them for so long.

Anderson said he was confident that he had a squad that would win more silverware in the very near future and there were few who would argue.

The future looked bright; the future looked dark blue.

Chapter 20:
Billy Steel

BILLY STEEL WAS one of Scotland's greatest inside forwards who combined a brilliant footballing brain with a busy work ethic and an explosive shot. He was a genius, a maverick, an individual, a joker, the superstar of his day and was arguably the best player ever to play for Dundee Football Club. Signed for a world record fee that was unsurpassed by a Scottish club for over a decade, he brought with him a national interest in Dundee that had been previously unheard of and brought glory to Dens as the Dark Blues won their first silverware for over four decades just over twelve months after he arrived.

Born in the Stirlingshire village of Denny on May 1st 1923, Billy Steel started his professional career with Leicester City when they nipped in, in front of a host of clubs, to sign the sixteen-year-old but his spell at Filbert Street was short lived when the manager was sacked and no one remembered to renew the young Scot's contract.

After a short spell at Love Street as an amateur, Billy joined St Mirren's Renfrewshire neighbours Morton but his stint in Greenock was soon interrupted by the Second World War during which he turned out for the British Army on the Rhine. Re-establishing footballing connections with other teams on the Continent, the team visited France, Holland, Poland, Switzerland, the Channel Islands and Germany, and Steel played alongside such notables as Leslie Compton, Eddie Hapgood and Matt Busby before being demobbed in December 1946, when he returned to Morton.

In 1947, Billy enhanced his growing reputation when he was selected to play for Great Britain against The Rest of Europe at Hampden Park in Glasgow and he turned in a star performance, scoring Britain's third goal in a 6-1 win. His place as one of the game's rising stars was now assured and Billy decided to try his luck south of the border once more when Derby County were persuaded to part with a then British record £15,500 for his signature later that year.

By September 1950, 'The Pocket Dynamo' had developed into one of the first football superstars who, with seventeen Scottish caps in his locker, was determined to earn enough money from the game to make him financially secure by the time he had retired from playing. His wife however was by then homesick and Billy moved back to Glasgow with her, only travelling down to Derby on match days, but it was an arrangement that was never going to work. As he started to attract interest from clubs north of the border, Billy took the unprecedented step of calling his own press conference to announce that he would be leaving Derby and it looked odds on that he would be going to boyhood heroes Rangers when he started using training facilities at Ibrox.

What the press didn't know however was that Dundee manager George Anderson had been secretly working on a deal to bring him to Dens and once Billy met the flamboyant Dark Blues boss, he was convinced that Dens Park was the place for him. Steel remembered an act of kindness Anderson had once shown him during the war, when he had organised some food and drink for the train journey home after playing in a five-a-side competition in the Granite City and so was happy to shake hands on a move with the bowler-hatted gentleman.

The genial Aberdonian was a highly persuasive character and on September 21st 1950, Dundee F.C. called a press conference where a beaming Anderson stunned the assembled media by declaring: *"Gentlemen, I want to introduce you to Billy Steel, ex-Derby County and now of Dundee!"* The country was shocked as the club had paid a world record fee of £23,500 for one of the best known players in British football and it was one of the transfer coups of the century.

Two days later, 34,000 fans, around 8,000 more than normal, turned out for Steel's debut against Aberdeen and while the flaxen-haired forward clearly lacked match practice, his clever positioning and masterly touches were an inspiration. With only nineteen minutes remaining, Steel became an instant hero to his new adoring public when he scored Dundee's opener with a low shot and the extinct volcano known as The Law which overlooks the ground almost erupted with the noise.

'Midget Gem' had been an automatic choice for Scotland since 1947 and further caps against Wales and Northern Ireland that autumn made Billy Dundee's first full internationalist since Colin McNab's Wembley appearance against England in April 1932.

The stocky inside-forward brought power and imagination to the Dundee front-line and by mid-November, they led the Scottish League 'A' Division with only one defeat in ten matches. Dundee continued their challenge for the league title and eventually finished third in April but the real glory was to come six months later and Billy was at the very heart of it.

'Budgem' as his team mates nicknamed him had outstanding ability which gave him a confidence which was often seen as arrogance and wasn't welcomed by his fellow players. He had a sharp tongue, which his team mates often found themselves on the wrong end of during the ninety minutes, but the impact he made on the park brought them the success that had slipped from their grasp in previous years.

The first of those successes came in October 1951 when Dundee beat Rangers 3-2 to lift the Scottish League Cup with Billy setting up skipper Alfie Boyd for the winner. Steel was a genius and he knew it and when Dundee won a free kick with only seconds remaining, after Rangers had just drawn level, Billy told Boyd to get in the box, saying to him, *"I'll place it on your head Alfie,"* and he did just that as Boyd leapt high to head home from eight yards out from Billy's high centre.

By the end of the season, Steel had scored six goals on a second 'Road to Hampden' but this time Dundee lost out 4-0 to Motherwell in the Scottish Cup Final. Six months later however, they were back on the Hampden trail and became the first side to retain the League Cup when Kilmarnock were put to the sword 2-0, with Billy scoring another six en route to the final.

Steel earned three League caps and thirteen full caps during his time at Dens and in one of those appearances became the first Scotland player to be sent off in May 1951. Billy took umbrage at the treatment dished out to his good friend George Young of Rangers and sought retribution against one of the offending Austrians in a match which became known as the 'Battle of Vienna'.

His time at Dens lasted four glorious years and his departure from Dundee was in typical Steel fashion when he called another press conference and shocked Scottish football by announcing he was emigrating to the United States. Steel saw out the rest of his days in America where he managed the Los Angeles Danes before taking a job in advertising after retiring and where he sadly died aged just fifty-nine in May 1982.

Billy Steel, 'Mr. Perpetual Motion' will never be forgotten at Dens Park where a hospitality lounge and supporters club bear his name and in May 2009, he was inducted into the inaugural Dundee F.C. Hall of Fame, having already been inducted into the S.F.A Hall of Fame three years before.

Steel was a hard little man with bounding vitality who as a perfectionist often did not suffer the short comings of less gifted colleagues, but he was adored on the Dens Park terracing and prior to Claudio Caniggia joining the club fifty years later, no Dundee signing had captured the public imagination and national headlines quite like Billy Steel's record-breaking move to Dens.

Honours at Dundee:

Scottish League Cup winners:	1951/52, 1952/53
Scottish Cup runners-up:	1952
Scotland full caps:	13
Scottish League caps:	3
Dundee F.C. Hall of Fame:	2009 Legends Award

Appearances, Goals:

League:	94, 27 goals
Scottish Cup:	13, 7 goals
League Cup:	24, 11 goals
Totals:	131, 45 goals

Chapter 21:
Scottish League 'C' Division
Champions 1951/52

SEASON 1951/52 MAY have been a major success with the League Cup win and the Scottish Cup Final appearance but the club had another success that year when they also won the Scottish League 'C' Division.

When the Scottish League was revived after the Second World War in 1946, it had intended to revert to its pre-war set-up of two divisions of twenty and eighteen clubs, just as the English League had done. However, many of the top tier sides preferred to retain the 16-14 club divisions that was used by the Southern League during the previous season and intended to break away and form a rival Super League if their wishes weren't granted. After much debate the League voted to keep the status quo and placed the six excluded clubs into a third division with the divisions being renamed A-B-C instead of 1, 2 and 3.

Of all the pre-war clubs, only two failed to restart, namely King's Park and St Bernard's. Stirling Albion were formed therefore as a replacement for King's Park, whose ground was destroyed in a bombing raid, while St Bernard's folded after their ground was sold from beneath them.

Three reserve sides therefore were invited to help make the number of member clubs up to ten and the reserve 'A' sides from Dundee FC, Dundee United and St Johnstone joined the new 'C' Division.

Only first teams could gain promotion to the 'B' Division and in the inaugural year of the 'C' Division, new club Stirling Albion pipped the Dundee reserves to the title and promotion as well as also beating Dundee 'A' in the final of the 'C' Division League Cup. As 'C' Division sides were excluded from the League Cup proper, they had to play in their own competition (which was played as a Supplementary League from 1947/48) and in its first year Stirling Albion beat Dundee 'A' 6-1 in the final at Annfield Park to earn them a unique double.

During the next couple of years, reserve teams of other top tier sides joined the 'C' Division and when the Scottish Reserve League was merged with the 'C' Division in 1949 to create two regionalised sections, it became almost well nigh impossible for other sides to achieve promotion as the minnows had to face the second strings of the 'A' Division giants. The League was known by many as the 'Cinderella of Scottish Football". Whereas no reserve sides won the 'C' Division between 1946 and 1949, they only failed to win it on one occasion after this and in season 1951/52 it was the Dundee reserve side who were the champions, finishing just ahead of Hearts in second.

Dundee's results 'C' Division results for season 1951/52 were as follows:

Aug 11th	Celtic 'A' (h)	won 4-1
Aug 15th	Aberdeen 'A' (a)	won 2-0
Aug 18th	Dunfermline 'A' (a)	won 6-3
Aug 22nd	Falkirk 'A' (a)	won 2-1
Aug 24th	Dundee Utd 'A' (a)	drew 3-3
Aug 29th	Hearts 'A' (h)	won 3-0
Sep 1st	Raith Rovers 'A' (h)	won 5-1
Sep 8th	Berwick Rangers (h)	drew 3-3
Sep 15th	Stirling Alb 'A' (a)	lost 3-1
Oct 1st	Raith Rovers 'A' (a)	drew 3-3
Oct 13th	Falkirk 'A' (h)	won 2-1
Oct 27th	Brechin City (h)	drew 1-1
Nov 3rd	Montrose (a)	won 2-1
Nov 10th	Aberdeen 'A' (h)	won 6-0
Nov 17th	East Fife 'A' (a)	won 3-1
Oct 20th	Hearts 'A' (a)	lost 7-1
Dec 1st	Leith Athletic (a)	won 2-1
Dec 8th	Brechin City (a)	won 5-3
Dec 15th	Dundee Utd 'A' (h)	won 5-2
Dec 22nd	Berwick Rangers (a)	lost 3-2
Dec 29th	Dunfermline 'A' (h)	won 3-0
Jan 2nd	St Johnstone 'A' (h)	won 11-0
Jan 12th	Leith Athletic (h)	won 3-0
Jan 19th	Hibs 'A' (a)	lost 2-1
Feb 9th	East Fife 'A' (h)	won 4-0
Mar 15th	Montrose (h)	won 3-0
Apr 19th	St Johnstone 'A' (a)	won 2-1
Apr 21st	Stirling Alb 'A' (h)	lost 2-1
Apr 23rd	Hibs 'A' (h)	won 4-0
Apr 26th	Celtic 'A' (a)	lost 3-0

Scottish League 'C' Division 1951/52
Final League Table

	P	W	D	L	F	A	Pts
Dundee 'A'	30	20	4	6	94	46	44
Heart of Midlothian 'A'	30	19	4	7	73	36	42
Hibernian 'A'	30	19	4	7	88	44	42
Celtic 'A'	30	19	3	8	68	49	41
Aberdeen 'A'	30	17	4	9	82	47	38
East Fife 'A'	30	15	5	10	66	57	35
St. Johnstone 'A'	30	14	5	11	66	71	33
Berwick Rangers	30	12	7	11	66	68	31
Stirling Albion 'A'	30	13	2	15	51	65	28
Raith Rovers 'A'	30	10	6	14	51	56	26
Brechin City	30	9	7	14	57	65	25
Dunfermline Athletic 'A'	30	10	5	15	57	72	25
Montose	30	10	5	15	47	69	25
Falkirk 'A'	30	8	2	20	65	85	18
Leith Athletic	30	5	7	18	46	88	17
Dundee United 'A'	30	3	4	23	35	94	10

The title was won on Wednesday April 23rd when Dundee 'A' defeated the reserves of the 'A' Division Champions Hibernian 4–0 at Dens with goals from Massie, Cowie and Henderson (2).

The Dundee team that played that night was: Carrie, Massie, Cowan, Ziesing, Merchant, Cowie, McGivrey, A. Henderson, Ewen, Williams, Hill with four of that side having been in the squad for the Scottish Cup Final four days earlier.

Perhaps of further satisfaction to those of a Dark Blue persuasion was the fact that the Dundee United reserve side finished bottom that season, making them officially the worst senior side in Scotland that year. Perhaps not unsurprisingly Dundee United withdrew from the 'C' Division after that but in the previous years there had been a number of entertaining, competitive 'wee derbies', which were often watched by crowds of several thousand.

Between 1946 and 1952, twelve competitive 'wee derbies' took place and the results were as follows:

"C" Division and "C" Divison League Cup derby matches:

Dundee A	6–1	Dundee United A	24/08/1946	C Division
Dundee United A	2–5	Dundee A	09/09/1946	C Division
Dundee United A	3–1	Dundee A	29/03/1947	C Division League Cup
Dundee A	2–2	Dundee United A	26/04/1947	C Division League Cup
Dundee A	2–1	Dundee United A	26/08/1949	C Division
Dundee United A	4–2	Dundee A	24/12/1949	C Division
Dundee A	1–1	Dundee United A	12/08/1950	C Division League Cup
Dundee United A	0–0	Dundee A	25/08/1950	C Division League Cup
Dundee A	5–0	Dundee United A	30/09/1950	C Division
Dundee United A	0–2	Dundee A	11/11/1950	C Division
Dundee United A	3–3	Dundee A	24/08/1951	C Division
Dundee A	5–2	Dundee United A	15/12/1951	C Division

Three years after becoming 'C' Division champions, Dundee and a number of other clubs intended to withdraw their reserve sides and reform the Reserve League and intimated this to the Scottish League at their AGM on June 12th 1955. The five 'C' Division clubs were therefore promoted to an expanded nineteen-club 'B' Division and the 'C' Division was abolished. The top two tiers were renamed Scottish League Division One and Two and the previous year's champions Aberdeen, with Dundee legend Bobby Wishart in their ranks, became the last club to win the Scottish League 'A' Division title.

Having won the 'B' Division in 1945/46 and in 1946/47, Dundee joined a small band of clubs who have won the top three divisions in Scotland (Hearts, Hibs and Dumbarton) when they became Scottish League Champions ten years after winning the 'C' Division and their third tier triumph in the same year as winning the League Cup showed the strength in depth that manager George Anderson could call upon.

Chapter 22:
George Christie

THE IDEA OF a player coming out of the Junior ranks to become a hero for Dundee was not a new experience for the club when Craig Robertson joined up for three games as a trialist from Lochee United in 2011, because exactly sixty years before, George Christie did just that and ended up winning two League Cup winners' medals. Christie joined the Dark Blues from Aberdeen Junior side Banks O' Dee in 1948 and ended up making 250 appearances over the next ten years, including three appearances in major cup finals at Hampden and scoring in a famous derby victory when Dundee put seven past United.

George made his debut for Dundee on November 18th 1950 away to Third Lanark and with Billy Steel having joined the club just eight weeks earlier, left winger Christie formed part of a new-look Dark Blue forward line. The following week, on his home debut, Christie scored twice in a 5-0 win over St Mirren and it was the first of his forty-seven goals that he would score over the next eight years.

Christie competed with Jimmy Andrews and George Hill for the left wing slot and when George started to establish himself in the side, 'Pud' Hill was switched to the right as Christie became the preferred partner for Steel on the left-wing.

On January 27th, George had his first taste of the Dundee derby when The Dark Blues drew 'B' Division Dundee United in the first round of the Scottish Cup at Dens but after being 2-0 up at half time, The Dee unaccountably relaxed and had to settle for a 2-2 draw. George was dropped in favour of Hill for the replay in which Billy Steel scored the only goal at Tannadice on a Wednesday afternoon four days later, but he was back in the side for Dundee's next match away to St Johnstone in the second round.

A record crowd of 29,972 packed into Muirton Park for Dundee's tie against another 'B' Division side and after former Dens Parker Jack Malloch gave Saints an early lead, an Alfie Boyd penalty and then counters from Christie and Ernie Ewen gave George Anderson's team a 3-1 win.

The Scottish Cup dream ended in the quarter-final at home to Raith in March when Christie's goal couldn't prevent Rovers winning 2-1 but there was to be cup glory for George and Dundee just a few months later, when they went all the way to the League Cup Final and defeated Rangers 3-2 in one of the most dramatic finals ever played at in Mount Florida.

The 1951/52 season kicked off with the League Cup sectional ties and Christie came into the side for the fifth tie against Hearts at Tynecastle after Jimmy Andrews had started the season on the left wing. In the next match at Stark's Park, Dundee gained a modicum of revenge for that Scottish Cup defeat to Raith by winning 3-1 and George was again on the scoresheet, this time with a brace.

Dundee scraped through the section on seven points ahead of Hearts on goal average and George was now an ever present en route to the final. He played in both legs of the 2-1 quarter-final aggregate win over Falkirk, and in the semi-final against Motherwell at Ibrox, Christie opened the scoring as

Dundee surged to a 5-1 win. Three late goals from Dundee gave the scoreline a more flattering look than the passage of play deserved but The Dee cared not a jot as they were in their first major final in twenty-five years.

In the final, Dundee would meet Rangers who boasted no fewer than eight Scottish internationalists but The Dark Blues could go into the game with confidence having beaten the Ibrox side 1-0 at Dens four weeks earlier. The week before the final, Dundee defeated Celtic at Dens 2-1 with George scoring the first and the side that lined up in front of 92,325 was the same as the semi-final win with Christie and Steel on the left.

Both of those players were to have a major bearing on the game as they were to be involved in setting up goals at crucial times. Despite Dundee controlling most of the early first half play, Rangers took the lead in twenty-one minutes, but just two minutes after the interval Dundee got their just rewards and drew level when Bobby Flavell fired home a Christie cross.

After being pegged back twice, Dundee would get a last minute winner to send the Dark Blue fans into delirium. They partied like they hadn't partied for years and huge crowds gave the players a rousing reception when they arrived back home.

A month after the final Jimmy Andrews joined West Ham for £10,000 after being unable to dislodge Christie from the left-wing berth and George now made that position his own.

On January 2nd, Dundee met Rangers for the third time that season and made it a hat-trick of wins with a 2-1 victory at Ibrox and it was a memorable afternoon for George when he scored the winner after Steel had pulled Dundee back on level terms.

That same month Dundee embarked on another 'Road to Hampden', this time in the Scottish Cup and they made it all the way to their second final of the season after dispatching Ayr United 4-0 at Dens in the first round. Christie was an ever-present throughout the Scottish Cup campaign and in the second round away to non-league Wigtown, he scored in a more than comfortable 7-1 win.

The campaign however was to ultimately end in disappointment as Motherwell were to run out 4-0 winners in the final in a scoreline that reversely flattered the Steelmen in the same way Dundee's victory in the League Cup semi had done.

It meant a Scottish Cup runners-up medal for George to add to his League Cup winners' one from earlier in the season but just six months later George added another winners' medal to his collection when Dundee successfully defended their League Cup.

Their defence of the League Cup started with a sectional win over Raith Rovers at Dens and Christie started the new season by scoring the winner against the men from Fife.

This time Dundee qualified comfortably from their section and in their nine games on the way to the final against 'B' Division Kilmarnock, Christie was an ever-present and took his usual number eleven shirt for the final against the Rugby Park men.

Dundee were strong favourites to lift their second League Cup but Killie belied their lower league status and took the game to Dundee from the off. George injured his shoulder in the first half and needed a pain killing injection at half time and nearly gave Dundee the lead with his long range shot fisted onto the bar by Niven just after the rbeak. His dashing runs down the wing were now starting to cause Kilmarnock problems and within the final eight minutes Bobby Flavell grabbed a double to win the cup.

Again there were joyous scenes amongst players and fans but their celebrations were curtailed a little due to a sudden downpour of rain. Fireworks, bugles and whistles however greeted George and his team mates when they returned to the city when they again went on a tour of the city on top of a bus with George's shoulder injury almost preventing him from climbing on top. He was one of an elite group of seven who had played in both winning finals and who are the only Dundee players to have won two major trophies with The Dee.

At the end of the season, Christie was part of a sixteen-strong party who went on a two-month long trip to South Africa where they played a marathon seventeen-strong schedule. In those games, Dundee won fifteen, drew one and lost one to the South African national side and George was on target nine times.

The following season however was a bit of a disappointment and started off poorly with the Dark Blues failing to get out of their League Cup section as Partick Thistle went through on goal average. The season ended on a high however with a 6-0 win over Jags in the final league game and seven days later, George was on target in a 9-3 win against Dundee United in a joint testimonial for Dundee's Jimmy Toner and United's George Grant.

If such large score in a testimonial means little in the grand scheme of things, then Dundee made it count when it really mattered when they put seven past their nearest rivals in a League Cup quarter-final tie at Dens on September 12th 1955. George got one of the goals in a 7-3 win on a day in which Jimmy Chalmers was the hat-trick hero. The match has been immortalised in the famous Johnnie Scobie song still belted out today where The Dees sing, *"So I went along to Dens Park, to see the famous eleven, and when we got there, the terracing was bare, but we gave United seven!"*

With United languishing in the lower league in those day, derbies were few and far between but in his time at Dens, Christie was involved in four winning derbies and one draw, scoring once.

In his last year with Dundee, season 1957/58, one of those derby wins was a 1-0 Forfarshire Cup victory at Tannadice but in his last game for The Dark Blues, a much bigger scalp was claimed when Rangers were defeated 1-0 at Ibrox just a few weeks after they had defeated Celtic 5-3 at Dens.

His last goal for Dundee came the week before that Celtic win when he scored in a 7-2 victory over Queen of the South in Dumfries and the hero that day was youngster Alan Cousin who grabbed a hat-trick as well at the winner at Ibrox on the final day.

Changes were taking place at Dens as manager Willie Thornton was starting to blood the youngsters and that season saw 1962 Championship winners Alan Cousin, Alex Hamilton, George McGeachie, Pat Liney, Hugh Robertson, Alan Gilzean and Bobby Cox all make their mark. Thornton's babes were starting to grab the headlines and many of the old guard were being moved on and Christie was shipped out to Third Lanark in the summer.

In later years George would move back to his native North-East and managed Deveronvale in the Highland League where he signed future Dee Kevin Bremner from schools football and he sadly died in Aberdeen aged eighty in January 2008.

Christie played in a golden age at Dens where victories over the Old Firm and winning cups were the norm and alongside team mate Jimmy Toner, he made the step up from Junior football to become a darling amongst the Dens Park masses.

Honours at Dundee:	
Scottish League Cup winners:	1951/52, 1952/53
Scottish Cup runners-up:	1952
Appearances, Goals:	
League:	184, 31 goals
Scottish Cup:	18, 3 goals
League Cup:	48, 13 goals
Totals:	250, 47 goals

Chapter 23:
Defending Their Honour

ON THE LAST day of the 1951/52 season Jimmy Toner, George Hill and Albert Henderson re-signed for the following year and in a summer clear-out no fewer than eleven players were released. Players with first team experience such as Ewen, Williams, Fraser and Beaton were freed while Basil Wilson returned to his homeland of South Africa having failed to make it into the first XI in his ten months at Dens.

After such a long season the previous year, with the trip to Turkey and Israel and participation in the St Mungo's Cup last summer, George Anderson gave his troops an extended break and with no pre-season matches, the first chance the Dundee fans got to see their heroes was the annual trial on Monday August 4th.

Anderson sent out two sides with experimental line-ups and a 12,000 crowd braved the rain to watch Billy Steel score the winner as the Whites defeated the Blues 2-1. Alfie Boyd captained the Whites, while Tommy Gallacher skippered the Blues but on the first match of the season five days later, Gallacher was left out of the side and was replaced by the versatile Ken Ziesing.

For months now Gallacher had been in dispute with Anderson over bonus payments due from the 1951 tour of Turkey and he had been irked enough not to invite Anderson to his wedding the previous February. Now, despite captaining a side in the trial match, Gallacher was left out of the first match against Raith Rovers on August 9th.

Instead the mid-line who lined up against the Kirkcaldy side was Ziesing, Boyd and Cowie which was the same three who had played against Third Lanark in the last game of the previous season. Alfie Boyd and Doug Cowie switched positions however and Gerry Follon dropped out in favour of Gordon Frew at right-back.

The by now traditional League Cup seasonal opener was the first match of the 1952/53 Scottish League Cup and Dundee had been drawn in 'A' Division, Group D alongside Raith Rovers, Clyde and Airdrieonians. The game against Raith was the first in the defence of the trophy they had won at Hampden the previous season and Dundee kicked off as holders in the white kit they had worn in the Scottish Cup Final in April. It was the first time therefore that a club badge had been worn in a match at Dens and a healthy crowd of 20,000 turned up for the new campaign.

Dundee made a bright start to the new season with a 2-1 win against a side they had faced in the League Cup sectional ties last season. Goals from Burrell and Steel secured the win and after the match Anderson said he had had doubts about his new half-back line but they had not let him down. After a powerful display from the trio, the manager said his selection had been justified and would be chosen again at Airdrie four days later, who had opened their campaign with a 1-1 draw with Clyde at Shawfield.

The day before the match at Broomfield, Alfie Boyd got tonsillitis and the doctor ordered him to bed for twenty-four hours meaning that he would miss the Airdrie game. He was also to have an x-ray on a cartilage complaint and George Merchant was to come in to replace the skipper for his first ever League Cup match.

George who was nicknamed the 'Merchant of Menace' had made eleven appearances the season before deputising for Doug Cowie but later in his career he was changed from a defender to a centre-forward and was Dundee's top goalscorer in season 1954/55.

Against Airdrie he played at centre-half and was guilty alongside the rest of Dundee's defence of ballooning the ball upfield to the midget Dark Blue forward line who were brushed aside by the lanky Diamond defenders.

At half-time however there had been as serious confab amongst the Dundee players in the dressing room and from the start of the second half, every man made a point of keeping the ball on the ground. The forwards got the sort of service small forwards need with skill rather than robustness taking its rightful place.

Billy Steel was the man of the match and his dribbling, boundless energy and long, well judged passes ran the Lanarkshire defenders to a standstill. Steel's scheming and Flavell's opportunism were the complete second half victory story with Bobby getting a hat-trick against his former team.

His first came in the fifty-sixth minute when a perfect Steel inswinger was slickly headed home by Flavell and in seventy-nine minutes he made it two when he picked himself up in a scramble and slashed it home. The little centre completed his hat-trick in the last minute when he anticipated a pass-back by left-back Tom Brown and literally walked the ball past the helpless goalkeeper.

"It was a grand sporting game with Flavell getting a special cheer at the finish for his hat-trick," reported Jack Harkness in *The Courier* and it was a grand evening for Dundee with Raith beating Clyde 4-3 at Stark's Park to give Dundee a two-point lead at the top of their section.

Dundee's next match was against Clyde at Dens three days later and the Glasgow side were suffering from plenty of knocks from their midweek trip to Fife where they had been 3-0 up. Clyde were promoted as 'B' Division champions the previous season after just one year down in the second tier and their manager Paddy Travers, who had led the Bully Wee to Scottish Cup glory in 1939, delayed announcing his team until the Saturday morning.

For Dundee, Alfie Boyd was still out and so Merchant retained his place in the same eleven who had faced Airdrie. Just as it had been at Broomfield, there was a real contrast in height between the opposing forwards with Clyde's attackers averaging over 6ft and the Dark Blue attack averaging just 5ft 6ins.

Clyde started like a side who had no business being in the 'A' Division and were struggling under Dark Blue bombardment. After Dundee scored two good first half goals through Flavell and Steel however, they began moving at a leisurely pace, taking their foot off the gas and squandering chances and the Bully Wee sensed an opportunity to get back into the game.

In the second half the Shawfielders changed their ideas and their lanky forwards discovered nervousness in The Dee defence and in forty-nine minutes Buchanan scored when Merchant misjudged a high ball. A few minutes later Billy McPhail headed home an equaliser and, after throwing away a three-goal lead against Raith, came back from two goals down to earn a vital draw.

In fact Clyde were unlucky not to snatch a win when Tommy Ring had a goal chopped off and the Dundee players left the field at full time to a chorus of boos from the 21,000 crowd.

Perhaps with the future in mind, Anderson had tinkered with the side for the first three games but these changes did not go down well with the fans and Frew's form was adversely affected by the barracking. Follon and Gallacher were therefore recalled for the next match with Raith Rovers in Fife on August 23rd although for Gallacher it was in the unfamiliar position of inside-right after a series of fine performances in the reserves.

Dundee's draw with Clyde coupled with Raith's 1-0 win at Broomfield meant that the match at

Stark's Park was a potential section decider with a big crowd expected. Dundee were one point ahead of Rovers going into the match and for the visit of the holders, Raith manager Bert Herdman decided to move Willie Penman to the wing in an attempt to get the win they needed to keep their League Cup hopes alive. Penman was Rovers' second longest servant and had scored more than 300 goals in eleven seasons but Herdman felt that Penman could become provider and put pressure on Dundee's full-backs.

Alfie Boyd also came back into the match for Dundee, taking his number five shirt back from Merchant and his experience was vital in a bruising encounter. Boyd received a cut eyebrow on his comeback, Gerry Follon got a knock on the forehead which gave him slight concussion and impaired his sight, Gerry Burrell had a suspected fractured rib and Bobby Flavell was booked after a melee in the Raith penalty area with Colville. Bookings were so rare in football in the Fifties that the caution received a sub-headline in most of the newspapers on the Sunday.

What made the main headlines however was the reaction of Raith Rovers' directors who were to write to the Scottish League and S.F.A. to complain about the referee and ask for a replay after The Dee won 2-1 with a double from Steel. The Raith directors and manager expressed dissatisfaction with the handling of the game by referee J. Walker of Aberdeen and they wrote to both Scottish footballing bodies to ask that he not officiate any Raith Rovers game in the future.

They alleged that poor decisions cost Rovers the points and placed emphasis on two particular incidents in the Dundee goalmouth before Steel opened the scoring. Raith claimed that both Ziesing and Cowan handled in the penalty area and that spot kicks should have been awarded and further alleged that Gallacher had fouled a Raith player before Steel scored Dundee's winning goal.

The Raith directorate were aware that a referee supervisor was at the game and asked if it was in order for the Stark's Park club to have a copy of his report. *"There is nothing in the rules which says we should not have it,"* said Bert Herdman the following day. *"We want a copy. We want the Scottish League to deal with this and would have said nothing if we were beaten on merit."*

Rovers asked the Scottish League if their management committee would hear a deputation from the management of Raith Rovers F.C. and asked if the League would consider the possibility of the match with Dundee being replayed.

George Anderson was unconcerned and said, *"I'm sure the League and the S.F.A. will defend the honour of the officials,"* and in the event the Scottish League refused the deputation from Kirkcaldy and the 2-1 win for the Dark Blues stood.

The victory, while it did not guarantee Dundee passage into the next round, did put them into a very strong position and two days later, the Scottish League took the unusual step of making the draw for the quarter-finals before the group stages were finished. Dundee's section winners were drawn to play 'B' Division, Section B winners which were likely to be Stirling Albion who had carried all before them since the season start.

Stirling had so far played four, won four, which included a 6-2 win over Dundee United at Tannadice and in the end would top their group with five points to spare and would defeat United 6-1 in the return game at Annfield.

For Dundee to qualify they had to win one of their last two games and the first chance to do that was against Airdrie at Dens on Wednesday August 27th. Dundee's injured players were making good progress at the week wore on and in the end only Gerry Burrell didn't make it and was replaced by Jimmy Toner.

Toner had a fine game and got on the scoresheet in the 3-2 victory as Dundee won through to the quarter-finals. Airdrie had stunned their hosts in just eight minutes when their first visit into the Dundee half brought a goal but after a period of pressure and a series of misses from Flavell, Gallacher and Toner, Dundee were back on level terms six minutes before the break when Flavell headed in a Gallacher cross.

Right on the whistle Toner made it two when he pounced on a rebound from a Flavell shot and in fifty-four minutes it was 3-1 after a neat one-two between Flavell and Steel resulted in the centre firing home.

In one of their rare attacks Airdrie pulled one back just after the hour but they never looked like drawing level. The Toner-Gallacher wing caused all the Diamonds all sorts of problems with Tommy unlucky not to score a number of times and the majority of the 19,000 crowd went home happy with Dundee setting up a date with the Scottish League's youngest side.

Dundee were through with a game to spare and their last sectional match with Clyde, although meaning nothing to either side, was a thrilling 3-3 draw. Dundee wore a natty new strip of blue and white quartered jerseys and white shorts, which *The Courier* described as looking like a chess board, but soon found themselves 2-0 down at half-time. However, three goals in eight second half minutes from Christie, Boyd (pen) and Toner put Dundee ahead though Clyde got a deserved equaliser when McPhail headed home late on.

Dundee's completed section table was as follows:

Team	Pld	W	D	L	GF	GA	GAv	Pts
Dundee	6	4	2	0	15	10	1.50	10
Clyde	6	1	3	2	15	15	1.00	5
Raith Rovers	6	2	1	3	9	14	0.64	5
Airdrieonians	6	1	2	3	9	9	1.00	4

The Dark Blues finished the League Cup sectional games with the best record of any 'A' Division side, topping their group with ten points. Rangers won their section with nine points and League Champions Hibs won theirs with eight and Dundee were now confident of progressing further in the tournament as the unseeded draw had paired them with a 'B' Division side.

They started dreaming of Hampden again!

Chapter 24:
Bobby Henderson

DUNDEE FC HAVE always had a fine tradition of good goalkeepers over the years and Bobby Henderson certainly fits into that category winning the League Cup with The Dark Blues in 1952 and playing in the Scottish Cup Final the same year.

Bobby career 'between the sticks' started when he played in goal for the 69th (Glasgow) Boys' Brigade team where he was spotted by Junior side Glasgow Perthshire, based in the north of the city in Possilpark. It was from Perthshire that he joined Partick Thistle in 1937 and it was a dream come true for Bobby as he was a boyhood Jags' fan and had been a ball boy at Firhill.

Between 1937 and 1951, he turned out 324 times for Thistle and was quickly taken to the hearts of the Jags' fans as a local lad from Amisfield Road in Maryhill. He was chosen six times to be a Scotland reserve in his time at Firhill but unfortunately never won a cap. His greatest performance for the 'Maryhill Magyars' was in a Scottish Cup first round match against Hibs at Easter Road in 1950 when he repeatedly defied their 'Famous Five' forward line as Partick pulled off a shock 1-0 win.

Just over twelve months later in May 1950, he was on his way to Dens after he was surprisingly given a free transfer by the Jags and Dundee manager George Anderson signed him up a competition for youngster Bill Brown who had broken into the first team that year. Brown had taken over the first team goalkeeping duties from Johnny Lynch towards the end of the season and when Lynch was freed after settling a dispute, Anderson brought Henderson in to replace him.

There was much speculation in the press as to who would start the 1951/52 season as Dundee's No. 1 and on August 11th it was Henderson who was given the nod and made his Dark Blue debut against St Mirren in Paisley in a League Cup sectional tie. The game finished 2-2 after Dundee had been 2-0 up and Henderson kept his place to make his home debut against Hearts four days later.

Bobby's first clean sheet for Dundee came in the next League Cup tie in a 5-0 home win over Raith Rovers but after a defeat to St Mirren in the next match, the Dark Blues themselves let in five in a 5-2 defeat in the return match with Hearts at Tynecastle.

With Dundee's qualification from their League Cup section hanging in the balance, Anderson made four changes for the last match at Stark's Park and Henderson was one of those dropped and was replaced by Brown.

It was a move which paid dividends as Dundee won 3-1 against Raith to top their group and with Brown getting plaudits for his performance, which including saving a penalty at 0-0, he kept his place in the side when the league campaign kicked off seven days later at Stirling.

Unfortunately for Bobby this meant that he would miss out on a League Cup winners' medal when Dundee went all the way in the competition with Brown in goal. He made a couple of appearances in the team when Brown was injured but was unable to reclaim the number one jersey permanently starting until a Scottish Cup first round tie against Ayr in January when Brown was called up for his National Service.

Dundee had hoped that Brown would be given permission to play in the game by the R.A.F. but they turned down the Dark Blues' request and Brown did not play again for The Dee for another twelve months. This meant that Bobby lined up in every match until the end of the season, including every game in a Scottish Cup run which took Dundee all the way to Hampden for the second time in six months.

Henderson was hoping to make up for missing the League Cup Final with a Scottish Cup winners' medal but it wasn't to be as Motherwell ran out 4-0 winners to take the trophy back to Lanarkshire.

Bobby wasn't very tall for a goalkeeper but his handling and reflexes were second to none and his popularity at Dens began to grow as the season progressed. When the new campaign in August, Henderson was still first choice keeper and in the traditional League Cup openers, played in all six group matches against Clyde, Raith and Airdrie as Dundee won their group at a canter.

After dispatching 'B' Division Stirling Albion over two legs in the quarter-final, Dundee were up against League Champions Hibernian in the semi-final and Henderson produced another fabulous performance against their 'Famous Five' forward line to help Dundee secure a 2-1 win and a trip to Hampden for the third cup final in a row.

He had played in every match on 'The Road to Hampden' and it was a chance for Bobby to put the disappointments of the last two behind him by this time picking up a winners' medal.

Standing between him and the winners' podium was 'B' Division Kilmarnock and it soon became evident that the Ayrshire part-timers were not just there to make up the numbers. Backed by a swirling Hampden breeze and roared on by their fans in the 51,000 crowd, they gave Dundee a first half pounding and it was largely thanks to an inspired display by Bobby Henderson that the score remained 0-0 at the interval.

The pattern continued in the second half with ten minutes left, Dundee got the vital breakthrough when Jimmy Toner sent a perfect pass through to Bobby Flavell who fired low past Niven to give Dundee the lead. Six minutes later Dundee made certain when Bobby's long kick from hand reached the Killie penalty area and as centre-half Thyne hesitated, Flavell raced in and thumped the bouncing ball into the corner of the net.

The game finished 2-0 and Dundee were League Cup winners for the second time in twelve months. Bobby at last got his winners' medal with a terrific display and an assist to boot and now looked to cement his position as Dundee's number one.

In the New Year however Bill Brown was available again and he shared the goalkeeping duties with Henderson for the rest of the season while still completing his National Service. His experience stood Bobby in good stead in season 1952/53 as he let in fewer goals than any other regular goalkeeper in Scotland.

Brown wasn't available to go on the two month end of season tour to South Africa, allowing Bobby to be first choice keeper on the trip but at the start of the new season, Brown was back in possession of the yellow jersey meaning Bobby would only play ten times that year.

It was much the same for season 1954/55 with Bobby only appearing twice and then only four times the year after and at the end of the season was given a free transfer by manager Willie Thornton, who had taken over from George Anderson in the summer of 1954.

In his final season, Henderson came back into the side for a Scottish Cup fifth round tie with Dundee United and after a 2-2 draw at a snow covered Tannadice, he kept his place for the 3-0 replay win at Dens four days later.

That game was his penultimate appearance for The Dee and by coincidence he made the shortest walk in football when he left the Dark Blues to sign up for 'B' Division Dundee United who were now managed by Bobby's former Dens Park trainer Reggie Smith.

He made his debut for United on August 11th 1956 in a League Cup tie at home to Ayr United but unfortunately for Bobby his Tannadice career was restricted to just ten matches after he broke his leg against Arbroath on September 5th. The game against the 'Red Litchies' was United's last League Cup sectional tie when they qualified with a 5-0 win but in the quarter-final they drew Dundee and badly missed Bobby's experience as they went down 7-3 at Dens.

Bobby made just one more appearance for United in a 5-1 defeat away to Albion Rovers and at the end of the following year decided to hand up his gloves. After retiring he would regularly go and watch his beloved Partick Thistle but would also proudly boast of winning the League Cup with Dundee and sadly died in May 2006 aged eighty.

At Dundee he kept nineteen clean sheets in seventy-five appearances and had the honour of keeping goal for Dundee in two cup finals at Hampden in front of almost 190,000 fans; a feat that no other goalkeeper in the history of Dundee Football Club can claim.

Honours at Dundee:

Scottish League Cup winners:	1952/53
Scottish Cup runners-up:	1952

Appearances:

League:	52
Scottish Cup:	8
League Cup:	15
Total:	75

Chapter 25:
Drawn and Nearly Quartered

DUNDEE CRUISED THROUGH to the 1952 Scottish League Cup quarter-finals where they had drawn Stirling Albion, but before that two-legged tie, the Dark Blues opened their league campaign against Motherwell at Dens on September 6th.

It was the chance for the Dark Blues to gain some revenge for the Scottish Cup Final defeat in April but with Dundee wearing their new blue and white chequered shirt, it turned out to be a dreadfully boring game that finished 0-0. Tommy Gallacher missed out after picking up an injury against Clyde as did Billy Steel who got a shoulder knock and after an x-ray it was decided to rest Billy for the 'Well game as any further knock could keep him out for over a month.

Before the next match George Anderson was taken into an Aberdeen nursing home suffering from pleurisy and although no operation was required, he was told to have a complete rest for at least a fortnight. Reggie Smith was therefore put in charge of team affairs with Reuben Bennett his assistant and the pair's first game at the helm was the League Cup quarter-final first leg match at Annfield on Saturday September 13th.

Twenty-four hours before that the Scottish League made the draw for the semi-finals and the ties were Rangers or Third Lanark v St. Johnstone or Kilmarnock and Morton or Hibernian v Stirling Albion or Dundee. The first semi-final was to definitely be at Hampden regardless of who was playing while the second semi was to be at Ibrox if Morton got through and Tynecastle if Hibs won.

The day of the four quarter-finals was the day in which the Scottish League's new admission prices came into force and for the first time in the League's history, there were to be different prices for the different divisions. The new prices were set at a minimum of 2s for the 'A' Division, 1s 9d for the 'B' Division and an unaltered price of 1s for the 'C' Division and these prices also applied to the League Cup. The minimum pricing meant clubs could charge more if they wanted but could not charge less and should a League Cup tie take place between sides from different divisions, as was the case of the Dundee v Stirling tie, then the prices would be set at the home club's standard.

The S.F.A. in response said that they might also set new prices for the Scottish Cup which the previous year were set at 1s minimum and were in discussions as to how to set prices when sides from two different divisions were drawn together.

Stirling were hoping that the new prices wouldn't adversely affect the gate and were looking forward to a big attendance at Annfield. They were to be missing inside-left George Dick through injury but had the 'B' Division's leading scorer George Henderson who had ten goals to his name already and were confident of pulling off a shock.

Dundee were equally confident of going through to the semis and had both Steel and Gallacher back from injury, with Gallacher returning to his more familiar position of right-half. Steel looked in the mood at the start making repeated darting runs at the Albion box and Dundee should have been 2-0 ahead after five minutes when Flavell missed two gilt-edged chances.

However, after quarter of an hour, Gallacher picked up a leg knock and his timing became faulty and Albion soon noticed this defensive weakness. They hit Dundee's right side hard and often and as Dundee's defence rolled back, the whole team became a disjointed lot.

Albion's schemer in chief was Johnny Smith who had been capped three times for Scotland as a Junior and he gave Stirling a deserved lead just before the interval. In the second half the 'Binos' continued to push forward and went two ahead through left-half Jim Fleming who was having a fine game. He cleared his lines effectively, turned defence into attack and oozed fighting spirit which his team mates were showing in abundance.

Gerry Burrell pulled once back for Dundee after being set up by Steel but Stirling restored their two-goal lead shortly afterwards and held out for a superb 3-1 win which simply stunned their top tier opponents.

Stirling had pulled off a huge shock against the holders and manager Tom Ferguson was understandably delighted. *"We had something that Dundee didn't have,"* he beamed afterwards. *"We had fighting spirit. What we have we hold and Dens Park holds no terrors for us and we will field the same team on Wednesday for the second leg."*

Dundee's hold on their League Cup was tentative at best and they would have to overcome a two-goal deficit to stay in the competition. It had been a bad start for the temporary management team of Smith and Bennett and never before had Dundee had to come back from two goals down after a first leg.

The only other times the sides had met before in the League Cup had been in the 1945/46 sectional ties when both clubs were in the 'B' Division and after Stirling won 2-0 at Annfield in the first game, Dundee blew the 'Binos' away 8-1 in the return sectional match. Both Gerry Follon and Dundee's assistant Rueben Bennett played in those matches six years before and they were hoping for a similar outcome this time.

The Courier said it was *"a formidable task but one that shouldn't be beyond the Dark Blues"*. Reggie Smith made three changes in an attempt to get into the semis. Doug Cowie returned at left-half after injury, Jimmy Toner came in at outside-right and Ken Ziesing switched from left-half to right-half while Tommy Gallacher and Gerry Burrell dropped out.

A superb 24,000 turned up, 1,500 of whom had come through from Stirling and they saw Dundee get off to the best possible start with a goal from Bobby Flavell in the third minute. It was Bobby's tenacity that won the counter when, after losing the ball to Norman Christie in the tackle, he refused to give up, regained possession and shot into the net.

It was the perfect start for Dundee but they were still one behind on aggregate and for the next half hour or so, continued to pound forward with the strong sun and wind behind them. Stirling had the ball in the net when George Henderson punched a cross into the goal but referee Mr W. Brittle spotted the offence with howls of consternation ringing in his ears from the terracing.

Dundee eventually the goal their pressure deserved. It came on thirty-four minutes after Flavell had the ball in the middle of the box and lost it but it ran to Steel and without a moment's hesitation, he fired it into the net.

It was 2-0 to Dundee at half-time meaning the tie was level and the feeling in the stadium was that Dundee should have scored more goals with the elements. Would Stirling – who had fought well throughout – now take advantage of the wind and pull off a memorable result in the second half?

Any hopes they had of pulling off a shock faded just thirty seconds after the restart when a Steel goal was greeted by an ear-splitting roar from the Dens Park terracing. It came after a George Christie cross was only half cleared and went straight to Billy who shot into the far corner of the net past the unsighted Jenkins to put Dundee 4-3 ahead on aggregate.

The Stirling heads dropped and never really looked like scoring and with ten minutes left Flavell made it 4-0 with the kind of goal strikers dream about. Toner gave him the ball on the half-way line before he beat Christie and ran the length of the half with the Stirling defence in pursuit. As he reached the box, Bobby was tackled by Christie in front of the onrushing Jenkins but he managed to get his shot in which just rolled over the line.

With the last kick of the night, Dundee made it five when Toner was fouled in the box and Alfie Boyd thumped home the spot kick. It finished 5-0 and after a major scare, Dundee were through to the semi-finals. Billy Steel had been at his international best and Bobby Flavell had looked dangerous from the off but the most pleasing display for the home support was the performance of inside-right Albert Henderson, who had made his debut in the first leg. He put in a power of running and in the last twenty minutes led most of the home attacks and had now staked his claim for a regular place in the side.

At the end of the match James Gellatly phoned manager George Anderson at his Aberdeen nursing home to give him the good news and in reply told his chairman that *"Never had such a tonic helped an ill man."* Anderson wanted out of the nursing home to help with the arrangements for the semi-final but his doctors weren't so keen and told him he needed a lot more than a week's rest. He had been running up a phone bill in the nursing home trying to deal with his confectionery business, town council business and business at Dens but Mr. Gellatly assured him it was all in hand and wished him a full and speedy recovery.

Dundee's semi-final opponents were to be reigning League Champions Hibernian who had impressively beaten Morton 12-3 on aggregate in the quarters (6-0 at Cappielow and 6-3 at Easter Road). It didn't get much tougher than that and because it was Hibs who had qualified, the match would be at Tynecastle and not Ibrox.

Dundee's recent record against Hibs wasn't good, without a win in three years and the previous season had lost 3-1 at Dens and 4-1 at Easter Road. The Dark Blues would have to be at their very best if they were to reach their second successive final.

It was announced on Friday that the match would be all ticket with a limit of a 48,000 capacity with 39,000 in the ground, 6,000 in the enclosure and 3,000 in the stand. The stand was to be split between Dundee, Hibs and the host club Hearts after the Scottish League took their share and Hearts manager Tommy Walker phoned Dens to ask how many tickets they wanted. Prices were set at centre stand 10s 6d, wing stands 5s, enclosure 3s and ground 2s and director Jack Swadel told Walker that Dundee would take *"As many as you've got."*

Seven special trains were to run between Dundee West and Haymarket stations to carry 3,500 fans and with the game being played on a Saturday, it was thought as many as five times that might travel from Juteopolis.

In Dundee's next league match against Aberdeen at Dens they again wore their new blue and white chequered shirts but supporters complained at full time that it was difficult to differentiate between the players because of *"the dazzle effect of the check"*. The players themselves also told Reggie Smith that they weren't keen on them and he agreed in George Anderson's absence that they wouldn't be seen again and would be consigned to history after only three games.

It had been Anderson's idea to introduce them but no one had the heart to tell him they had been binned and he wouldn't discover it until he saw a newspaper report of Dundee's next match against Clyde. At Shawfield, where they had first worn the checks, Dundee were back to their traditional dark blue which they had worn since their inaugural season in 1893. Dark blue had been the colours of Our Boys, one of the founding clubs of Dundee F.C., and they alternated in their first season with the sky blue and white vertical stripes of the other founding club, East End. In Dundee's second season however, they stuck with the dark blue shirts (and dark blue shorts – they first wore white shorts in 1902) with the colour soon becoming one of the club's nicknames. Many fans were glad to see the back of the blue and white chequered shirts.

Against Clyde on Saturday September 27th, Dundee drew 1-1 with George Christie on target and it was the third draw between the sides already that season. Their focus could now turn to the semi-final of the League Cup and the tickets went on sale for the match two days later at 5pm after a Dundee reserve match. Dundee had stated that no tickets would be on sale at the secretary's office in Reform Street and it had been hoped that selling them after a 'C' Division match might boost the crowd for a Monday afternoon.

Tickets were restricted to two per person for the stand or enclosure with no limit on ground tickets and by 5pm, a queue of around 2,000 people had formed. By 6pm however, only 5,000 briefs had been shifted and so an announcement was made that tickets would be available in Reform Street for the rest of the week.

Dundee also announced that they were to withdraw from the Forfarshire F.A. as they had difficultly fitting in matches in the Forfarshire Cup and Dewar Shield. While local cup competitions were once a source of pride and satisfaction, Dundee now had their eyes on much bigger prizes and would not return to the Forfarshire F.A. for four years.

In the build-up to the Hibs game, all players were told to report to Dens Park for full training. Since the start of the season some players had trained with clubs that were local to where they lived, with Billy Steel, George Christie, Bobby Henderson and Albert Henderson training at Firhill and a couple of players training on occasion at Pittodrie. This was decided after Reggie Smith and Reuben Bennett went to visit George Anderson in the nursing home in Aberdeen before the Clyde game when the plans for the semi-final were laid out.

On Tuesday 30th some players took part in the Footballers' Golf Cup at Cawdor near Glasgow and representing Dundee F.C. were Jimmy Toner, Alfie Boyd, Doug Cowie, Ernie Copland and Ken Ziesing. They were competing against East Fife, Hibs, St. Johnstone, Dunfermline and Aberdeen and with the best three scores of the five counting, the competition was won by Aberdeen with Dundee third behind Hibs.

There was also an auxiliary competition for managers, directors and coaches and Dundee were represented by Reggie Smith. This was won by former Dundee goalkeeper Jock Brown, trainer at Kilmarnock, who beat Smith by nine strokes and at the end of the day, Dundee's trainer made an astonishing prediction.

"We had a good day and although Hibernian and Kilmarnock may have beaten us in the golf cup today I am sure we can beat them both in the League Cup when it really matters."

This was astonishing because Kilmarnock were due to play Rangers in the second League Cup semi-final and the men from Ibrox were the overwhelming favourites as Killie currently sat bottom of the 'B' Division. If Dundee were lucky enough to beat a side they hadn't defeated since March 1949, the chances were that they would play Rangers and not Kilmarnock in the final.

There was good news for Dundee that day however when Billy Steel trained at Dens under the watchful eye of Rueben Bennett after he had missed the match at Shawfield. Steel had been troubled once again by his ankle but told Colin Glen of The Courier to bet his car that he would be taking the field at Tynecastle.

On Friday Steel was put through a strenuous session to prove himself fit and passed it with flying colours and another player to come through his try out was the in-form Albert Henderson who had recently had an attack of tonsillitis.

By evening time Dundee had sold 10,000 tickets with the office at Dens open until 7pm and an extra allocation of stand tickets already sold out by Thursday. British Rail therefore announced that they were to put on three additional football specials to take the number up to ten, though they warned in their newspaper adverts that these trains would be compartment only with no corridor.

Dundee themselves were travelling by train and were crossing the Tay Bridge, the longest rail bridge in Europe, at 11.15am. The tickets they had left had been sent through on the 8.40am train to allow them to be sold at Tynecastle and The Dark Blues themselves arrived in Gorgie just after half past one.

Barring their way to another Hampden appearance was probably the finest footballing side in Scotland at that time. Although Dundee had lost only once in eleven games, the Easter Road side were clear favourites, having already scored forty goals that season. One week earlier they had pulverised the much-fancied Motherwell 7-3 at Fir Park and their brilliant forward line of Smith, Johnstone, Reilly, Turnbull and Ormond fully merited their 'Famous Five' nickname.

However, Dundee had the currently the best defence in Scotland, having conceded two fewer than any other club and Tynecastle had been a happier hunting ground for The Dee than it had been for Hibs.

A win for Dundee would mean a second successive final and for Hibs it would be their second final in three years, having lost 3-0 to Motherwell in the 1950 final. Although they had won three league championships in the last five years, a cup win was distinctly lacking on their C.V.

Dundee's forward line was the same as had fired five against Stirling in the last round and it meant there was no place in the team for Tommy Gallacher. He had come back into the Clyde game at inside-right but now dropped out to allow Albert Henderson to come back in and it was a disappointed Tommy who lined up for the reserves at Dens.

George Anderson was still recovering in the nursing home but sent the Dundee players a telegram before the match which was read out by Reggie Smith: *"What we have we hold. Get in and make it five."* He planned to listen to the live second half commentary on the radio as it was the norm until the early Nineties to have only live commentary of the second forty-five in case it affected the crowd!

For the first half, Anderson arranged for telephone updates from Tynecastle and what he heard would not have helped his recuperation. In front of 44,200 Dundee dominated the early stages and Albert Henderson had two terrific shots which just whistled over the bar but it was Hibs who took the lead when Lawrie Riley put the Easter Road side ahead on the half hour.

Five minutes later it was very nearly two when Bobby Johnstone attempted a spectacular overhead kick which was so unexpected that it made the crowd gasp. It was speeding straight for goal but Bobby Henderson brilliantly tipped it round the post and Hibs went in at the interval 1-0 ahead.

At half-time Reggie Smith and Reuben Bennett gathered the players in the dressing room and told them that they were the better side and that Hibs were there for the taking and The Dark Blues went out for second half in determined mood.

Straight from the restart Dundee went out on the offensive and seven minutes after Anderson had switched on his wireless, Dundee were level thanks to clever passing between Flavell and Steel which ended with Billy knocking in from close range.

The tide had turned and led by the darting Steel and the dashing runs of Christie, Dundee went pushing on in an attempt to get a winner. Jimmy Toner jolted the Hibees when he hit the bar on the hour and from that moment on, he led the green and white defence a merry dance. He always seemed to be in the empty space to collect the passes of Ken Ziesing and throughout Ken was masterly in attack and defence.

Jack Cowan had had a tough job in the first half with Gordon Smith but he stuck with it and marked Smith out of the game in the second forty-five while Gerry Follon on the other side could take the credit for the ineffective play of Ormond and Turnbull.

Dundee were well on top and with just ten minutes left on the clock they got their reward when Flavell ended a goalmouth melee by crashing the ball past Tommy Younger for the winner. Dundee's copybook football had had Hibs chasing in vain and the Steel-Flavell double act had paid off with Steel in particular in breathtaking form.

Dundee were through to their third Hampden final in twelve months and Hibs manager told the press, *"There is no doubt about it but the better team won and I congratulate George Anderson to whom I send my best wishes."*

Anderson was understandably delighted, sending a telegram to the capital saying, *"I'm very proud of the boys."* Reggie Smith gave his boss his own version of the match over the telephone that evening once he returned to Dundee and the pair already started to discuss plans for the final in three weeks time.

It was a tremendous achievement to knock the League champs out to reach a hat-trick of finals and now the Dark Blues looked to become the first side to successfully defend the League Cup.

Chapter 26:
George Hill

GEORGE HILL WAS a dashing winger who did much to bring Dundee out of the wilderness at the end of the Second World War and into the forefront of Scottish Football. A provisional signing in 1939, he was a terrific servant to Dundee, remaining with the club until 1955 and he was part of one of the most successful periods in the Dark Blues' history.

As a player, 'Pud' as he was known, was way before his time and he could cross a ball with great accuracy and had an amazing burst of speed. Like many wingers of his age, he was small and had a bag of tricks on the ball and when 'Wee Hilly's' name was announced over the tannoy on a match day, the Dens Park crowd would roar with delight.

'Pud' signed for Andy Cunningham's Dundee in 1939 after scoring in a trial match for Arbroath against the Dark Blues and made his debut for The Dee in a Scottish War Cup tie against Third Lanark on February 24th 1940. He played nine times in the Scottish League Eastern Division before Dundee retired for the duration of the conflict during which he returned to his old club, Junior side Dundee North End.

George returned to Dens Park as soon as the club started up again in the Scottish League North Eastern Division in 1944 and missed just one match as Dundee won the First Series which was played from August to December.

When the Scottish League resumed properly the following season, Dundee were in the 'B' Division and had to win it two years in a row before getting promotion. In the second campaign George played twenty-two times scoring four goals.

Within two years Dundee were challenging for the Scottish League Championship and Hill was a key figure, scampering along Dundee's touchline and scoring five times in twenty-eight appearances, including the winner against defending champions Hibernian in a 4-3 victory at Easter Road.

On the last day of the season however Dundee failed to lift the League flag when they surprisingly flopped 4-1 at Falkirk but it could have been so different had Alec Stott converted a penalty at 0-0 after 'Pud' was brought down in the box at the end of a mazy run in which he beat three men.

Dundee did win some silverware in 1951 and 1952 when they twice won the Scottish League Cup but injury denied Hill a winner's medal both times. On the first 'Road to Hampden' George played once in the quarter-final second leg win over Falkirk but didn't played in any of the matches on the way to the '52 win.

George did however play in the 1952 Scottish Cup Final defeat to Motherwell and played in three of the matches en route and scored twice in the 7-1 second round victory over non-league Wigtown & Bladnoch. He missed the quarter and semi-finals with a broken arm but came back in for the final to replace the unlucky Gerry Burrell who had scored in the semi-final win over Third Lanark in Hill's absence.

By 1955 George Anderson had been replaced as Dundee manager by Willie Thornton and when

'Hill's outings began to be restricted because of a knee injury, Thornton allowed him to join East Fife after making 257 appearances for The Dee and scoring fifty times.

In 1956 he became manager of Montrose in the year they were admitted into the Scottish League and it was a position he enjoyed at Links Park for three years.

George was considered by many to be unfortunate not to be capped by his country and upon retiring from the game, he ran a newsagent in Dundee's east end. 'Pud' would often be seen in the Boars Rock bar in the city's Arbroath Road regaling regulars with stories about his days at Dens Park, playing alongside Billy Steel, until he sadly died in 2002 aged eighty-one.

Back in the days when football teams were clearly structured into eleven different positions, it was often the wingers who provided the greatest excitement and George Hill certainly did that during his sixteen years as a Dee. 'Pud' was an outstanding performer for Dundee and although small in stature, he lacked nothing in tenacity, and it was this, allied to his speed and ability, which made him a great favourite with the Dens Park fans.

Honours at Dundee:	
Scottish League Championship runners-up:	1948/49
Scottish Cup runners-up:	1952
Scottish League B Division winners:	1945/46, 1946/47
Scottish League North-East Division (First Series) winners:	1944/45
Appearances, Goals:	
League:	201, 42 goals
Scottish Cup:	15, 3 goals
League Cup:	35, 3 goals
Other:	6, 2 goals
Totals:	257, 50 goals

Chapter 27:
Creating a Record

DUNDEE F.C. WERE through to play in the 1952/53 Scottish League Cup Final but it wasn't the opponents they expecting after one of the biggest shocks in Scottish football history. While Dundee were beating Hibernian in the semi, Rangers were facing Kilmarnock at Hampden in the other tie and with the Ayrshire side currently rooted to the bottom of the 'B' Division, the Ibrox men were overwhelming favourites to make it two finals in a row.

Instead of setting up a date with Dundee however, in what would have been a repeat of the 1951 Final, Rangers succumbed to the Rugby Park part-timers with a freaky late goal from a free transfer in the last minute. Just as the crowd of 45,000 were preparing themselves for extra time, Killie's Willie Harvey sent over a harmless looking cross and instead of just clearing it, the Rangers' left back Johnny Little tried to trap the ball just yards from the goal line. As he struggled to get it under control, the alert Willie Jack came charging in and he managed to force the ball over the line to send Kilmarnock into their first ever League Cup final.

Jack had joined Kilmarnock on a month's trial the previous December after being freed by both Albion Rovers and St. Mirren and his goal propelled him into Rugby Park folklore.

Killie's all-round teamwork was a feather in the cap of manager Malky McDonald who laid down their pattern of play after having watched Rangers in their last two games. He had joined Kilmarnock in May 1950 to replace Alex Hastings and improved their position by ten points and seven places to a respectable fifth in his first season and even had to pull on his boots himself at the age of thirty-nine in an injury crisis. McDonald would lead Kilmarnock to promotion to the 'A' Division in 1953/54 and reaching the League Cup Final was terrific achievement in his second year in charge.

When Dundee and Kilmarnock met on October 25th 1952, it was the first time the sides had met since World War Two. Killie started the 1946/47 season in the 'A' Division with the Dark Blues in the league below and when Dundee won the 'B' Division, the Ayrshire club were one of the sides who were relegated. The only other side in Scottish football which Dundee hadn't met since the war was Hamilton Academical, who went down with the Rugby Park side. The last time Dundee had played Kilmarnock was January 29th 1938 and their 3-1 win in Ayrshire was a crucial for Killie as The Dark Blues went down at the end of the season in second bottom place, one point behind Kilmarnock.

Four days after Dundee's semi-final win over Hibs, Billy Steel played for the Scottish League against the League of Ireland at Celtic Park and scored Scotland's third from a Gordon Smith cross in the 5-1 win. His performance must have impressed the selectors as the following day he was called up for the full squad's match against Wales on October 18th with Doug Cowie being named as the reserve.

Dundee's next match was against Raith in the League and Alfie Boyd missed the 1-1 draw in Fife with his knee still sore after Tynecastle. Jimmy Toner also missed out with a slightly sprained muscle, with George Merchant coming in and the pair faced a race to be fit for the final in a fortnight's game.

Since losing to Raith two years ago in the Scottish Cup quarter-final, Dundee had played Rovers seven times and won the lot and an Albert Henderson strike continued that unbeaten run.

Watching the match at Starks Park was Kilmarnock manager Malky McDonald whose side were playing Dunfermline in Fife and he caught the team bus to East End Park before hitching his way to Kirkcaldy. Kilmarnock were the third 'B' Division side to reach the League Cup Final after East Fife in 1947 and 1949 and Raith Rovers in 1948 after watching the Dark Blues draw 1-1 at Starks Park was confident his side could emulate the Methil club's two victories.

The crowd was not expected to be big for the final but there was little opposition in Glasgow as Clyde v Hibs was the only other match scheduled to take place in Glasgow that day. Dundee had been due to play Rangers at Ibrox, Celtic were therefore away and Queens Park had to postpone their home match against Arbroath with their stadium hosting the Final.

The stand tickets went on sale at Dens on Thursday 16th October at 6pm and Dundee's 5000 allocation were to be restricted to two per person. Prices were 21s, 10s 6d, 7s 6d and 5s and entry to the north and south enclosures and the ground would be by cash. In just one day 16,000 stand tickets were sold between the clubs and the Scottish League, who now predicted that the crowd would be between 50 and 70,000. Dundee's continued to sell their stand tickets on Friday morning and *The Courier* were predicting 15,000 Dundonians would make the trip.

Bookings of buses in Dundee were heavy while every available coach in Ayrshire was hired and nine special trains were being laid on from Juteopolis by British Rail.

The week before the final Dundee faced Hearts in the league at Dens and Tynecastle director Frank McKenzie brought a gift for George Anderson who was unable to receive it in person as he was still recovering in a nursing home from pleurisy. The gift was a wooden plaque to hold his League Cup and 'B' Division winning medals and there was a special placed left for another winner's medal should Dundee beat Kilmarnock in seven days time.

Upon hearing about the plaque Dundee forward Bobby Flavell told the *People's Journal* that his 1951 medal was worn by his wife on a chain around her neck and he now wanted one for his daughter next week.

George Anderson wasn't the only member of the Dundee party to receive a gift as a fan anonymously left a sprig of white heather for captain Alfie Boyd at the main door at Dens. He had received an identical gift before the final twelve months previously and had worn it in his shorts when he scored the winning goal but as he didn't receive one before the Scottish Cup Final, he fully intended to wear it against Kilmarnock. Boyd would also have a rabbit's foot and a small piece of coal in his pocket and he hoped these traditional lucky charms would help him lift the cup aloft for a second time.

For the game against Hearts, Billy Steel was missing as he was playing for Scotland against Wales in a British Home Nations match and Jimmy Toner and Alfie Boyd came back into the side. Tommy Gallacher came in at inside-right for his first game in a month while Albert Henderson moved to inside-left to partner George Christie on that side.

It was a good test in the build up to the final with a 2-1 win thanks to goals from Cowie and Henderson. However just before the end Jack Cowan got a serious leg knock and although he finished the game, his leg was very painful. On Sunday he was sent for an x-ray and when it showed there was no fracture but only severe bruising on his ankle, Jack hoped to still make the final.

On Monday Cowan rested at home and was visited by club masseur Harry Easson at home and was told a decision would be taken on his fitness later in the week. The rest of the squad had to report to Dens on Monday morning to start cup final preparations, including the players who usually train elsewhere. Billy Steel was late, claiming problems with his train from Glasgow and did a full training session after reporting no ill effects from Scotland's 2-1 win in Cardiff.

There was good news for Doug Cowie when he arrived as he discovered that he had been chosen to play for the Scotland B team against France B in Toulouse on November 11th and after being in reserve on a number of occasions, he was now in line for his first cap.

There was also good news for George Anderson when he was granted permission to return home after making considerable progress in the last few days. In the evening Reggie Smith travelled to Aberdeen to meet with Anderson and discuss club affairs and the cup final preparations and Smith took with him the plague from Mr. McKenzie of Hearts. Anderson told Smith however that he still wasn't fit enough to travel to Glasgow at the weekend and made arrangements to receive phone calls from Hampden during the first half, while planning to listen to the second half commentary on the wireless, just as he had done for the semi.

On Tuesday Cowan still rested at home but the following day reported at Dens for treatment on his leg. The wet weather didn't hold up training for the rest of the squad as in the morning there was physical training done indoors and when the weather cleared, the players were out on the track.

Cowan's injury prevented the Dundee side being named but Kilmarnock unsurprisingly announced the same side that had defeated Rangers in the semi. Cup final fever was mounting in Ayrshire with shop windows full of blue and white rosettes, ties and scarves.

Whatever side Dundee named, the final was bound to be contested by two of the smallest forward lines in Scottish football with the biggest man was likely to be Dundee's Bert Henderson who was 5ft 8½ ins. Both forward lines were in form with Dundee having scored twenty-nine goals so far that season and Killie just two goals less and the press were salivating at the prospect of a high scoring game.

On Thursday Dundee named their side with Jack Cowan declared fit. Dundee named three changes from last year's winning team: Bobby Henderson was in goal with Bill Brown still on National Service, Albert Henderson was named at inside-right for Johnny Pattillo who was now Aberdeen's trainer and Ken Ziesing replaced Tommy Gallacher at right-half.

There was one positional change with a switch between Boyd and Cowie but for their old half back partner Gallacher, there was desperate disappointment. He had been in and out of the side since the start of the season and had played a number of games at inside-right instead of his more familiar right-half and was chosen to turn out for the reserves at Dens against Aberdeen on Saturday afternoon.

Tommy's ongoing dispute with George Anderson had perhaps cost him his place in the side and having played against Hearts the week before, he had high hopes of making Hampden. In *Dundee Greats* Gallacher told author Jim Hendry that *"I'd had a wee fall out with George Anderson over bonus payments during a close season tour of Turkey and I was still narked enough not to invite him to my wedding even though he was a good friend of my father, having played against him in goal for Aberdeen. I never liked playing for the reserves at any time but that was the worst. It was a bad memory for me."*

Despite his cup final snub, Gallacher still rated Anderson and also told Hendry *"He was a very astute man, brilliant at how he could handle players. He was years ahead of his time football-wise......a real shrewd cookie."*

After the players were informed of the team, skipper Alfie Boyd pinned a letter on the notice board in the home dressing room from Dundee Lord Provost William Black which read:

> *"Dear Mr. Boyd,*
> *"I understand that with your colleagues of the Dundee football team you are leaving for Glasgow on Friday.*
> *"Before you go I would like to extend to you and the members of the team my best wishes for victory against Kilmarnock on Saturday first.*
> *"I believe you have the opportunity of making history in this competition as no club has won this cup twice in successive years.*
> *"May I add that by your splendid play and by the conduct of all the members of the team, both on and off the field, you have brought credit not only to yourselves but to the city of Dundee.*
> *"With all good wishes,*
> *"Yours Sincerely,*
>   *William Black"*

Those who lived in Glasgow went home on Thursday afternoon on the 3pm train and were to meet up with the Dundee squad twenty-four hours later at the team hotel beside Buchannan Street when they arrived at on the corresponding Friday train.

Despite being named in the team on Thursday afternoon, Jack Cowan underwent a fitness test at Dens on Friday morning and after a severe try out it was decided he wasn't fit enough and would be too much of a risk to play in such a big game. It was a sad ending to an anxious week for Cowan who up to the last minute had been hoping to make a complete recovery from the ankle injury picked up against Hearts.

From the first it was serious but trainers Reggie Smith and Rueben Bennett and masseur Harry Easson did their best to get him fit throughout the week. In the end it was left up to Jack to decide he was fit enough and it was to his credit that declared that he would unable to play on Saturday.

Cowan was still to travel to Glasgow with the squad and told *The Courier* reporter at Dundee West station, *"I still feel a little pain when kicking the ball. Tomorrow I might be all right but there is a risk and I might let the side down. I will therefore not play."*

Cowan himself phoned manager George Anderson to tell him the bad news and then Anderson himself called Gordon Frew to give him the news that he would now be playing at Hampden. Frew was part-time at Dens and also worked as a chartered accountant in the city and was in his office when he received the call telling him he was playing.

Fate often plays strange tricks in football as twelve months previously Gordon Frew had played in all of Dundee's League Cup games up to the semi-final when Jack Cowan took over and retained his place in the final. Now this season, Cowan had been in possession of the number three jersey but injury cost the Canadian his place, with South African Frew taking over.

Frew's only first team appearances that season were in the first three League Cup section games at right-back alongside Cowan at left-back and now he was getting his chance of a cup winners medal.

"I am naturally happy to get the chance", said Gordon, *"but very sorry this has happened to Jack."*

After phoning Frew, Anderson then sent a telegram to the *Evening Telegraph* with the updated news and with a message to the Dundee supporters who were travelling to Glasgow on Saturday. It read:

> *"To the thousands who will be travelling again to Hampden, I hope you will see the real Dundee brand of*

football and enjoy the game. Then I also hope you will get the great thrills of last year's final when you returned home so happy."

Anderson then also sent a telegram to Dens with a message to the players and it was read out by Reggie Smith once they had boarded the train.

"To again reach the final you have overcome all hurdles. You have done this by producing football of real brilliance. You now face the last hurdle. I know that no matter how difficult, you will clear it and thereby create a record. Go to it boys! I'll be listening."

Dundee took with them to Glasgow 1300 unsold stand tickets and when they reached their hotel, they sent them by courier to the Scottish League headquarters in West Regent Street. The League were slightly vexed as they had been turning people away all week but expected them to sell out quickly on Saturday morning.

On Saturday morning, the exodus of fans started early with over 3500 travelling west with coach company W. Alexander while 120 fans were on buses from N.C.R. and another sixty from Dundee Gasworks. There was also a bus from the Dundee Mission to the Blind, ten of whom never miss a game while a group of war veterans organised a car pool from the British Legion.

Over 5000 supporters travelled by train; the first leaving for Glasgow at 8.10am with the 11.00am and 11.10am were going direct to Kings Park. For those terminating at Buchanan Street, a special Hampden service was being put on by the British Railways (Scottish Region) between Glasgow Central and Mount Florida with one train leaving every five minutes.

The players' wives and girlfriends were on the 10.10am departure and most of them picked up a copy of *The Courier* to read on the train so they could read a feature about themselves which had photos of each of the Dark Blue WAGs.

They met their partners for a light lunch with the players having postponed a short walk after breakfast because of the wet weather. After rising late from bed, the players instead played cards in the hotel lobby before heading up to Hampden around 1pm.

The Kilmarnock team assembled in Glasgow for lunch just as they did for any ordinary game and their whole week had been one of normal preparation. There were no special arrangements made back in Kilmarnock to greet the team should they return victorious but what they did have was a magnum of champagne tucked away in trainer Jock Brown's hamper as they didn't want to be caught napping should they upset the odds.

Win or lose the Killie team were to have dinner in the same Glasgow restaurant where they celebrated the defeat of Rangers in the semi three weeks before and although Dundee were hot favourites, there was a quiet confidence about the Rugby Park side.

By the time of the 2.30pm kick off there were 51,830 inside Hampden with blue the predominant colour on the terracing. There was a uniformity amongst the crowd with the majority wearing bunnets and demob suits; a three piece suit and waistcoat that servicemen were given when they were demobilised from the armed forces at the end of the Second World War.

As a large number of spectators smoked a pipe; large football crowds at this time often had a unique aroma and aura and Hampden in particular created its own special atmosphere on big match days. With an official capacity of 184,500, it was the largest football stadium in the world until the completion of the Maracana two years previously for the 1950 World Cup. The enthusiastic shouts from the spectators, the vast open terraces shaped like a bowl and the swirling winds combined to create a unique atmosphere known simply as the 'Hampden Roar' and when the teams came out the Dundee and Kilmarnock fans created their own version with gusto.

Coming out of the South Stand tunnel, Dundee were wearing their traditional dark blue shirts and white shorts while Kilmarnock wore their home colours of blue and white vertical stripes as the Scottish League had deemed that their kits did not clash.

The teams line up as follows (with positions in brackets):

Dundee: Bobby Henderson (gk), Gerry Follon (rb), Gordon Frew (lb), Ken Ziesing (rh), Alfie Boyd (ch) capt., Doug Cowie (lh), Jimmy Toner (rw), Albert Henderson (ir), Bobby Flavell (cf), Billy Steel (il), George Christie (rw).

Kilmarnock: John Niven (gk), Ralph Collins (rb), Jimmy Hood (lb), John Russell (rh), Bob Thyne (ch), Jim Middlemass (lh) capt., Tommy Henaughan (rw), Willie Harvey (ir), Gerry Mays (cf), Willie Jack (il), Matt Murray (lw).

Continual overnight rain had made the pitch heavy and the notorious Hampden wind was swirling strongly and when Jimmy Middlemass won the toss, he chose to attack the west goal with the wind in their favour. Straight away it was evident that the Ayrshire part-timers were not merely there to make up the numbers and took the game to Dundee and bombarded the Dark Blues' goal with a wave of attacks. It was a palpitating first half where Killie had Dundee at full stretch and only an inspired display of goalkeeping from Bobby Henderson kept the Killie attack at bay.

At the interval Dundee were lucky to still be on level terms but with wind advantage in the second half, they were hopeful of turning the tide.

The Dens defence had held up well but the attack had created little with youngster Bert Henderson badly affected by nerves and with Billy Steel closely marked by Johnny Russell, he was a shadow of his former self. The 'root' of the problem became clear a few days after the final however when Steel had no fewer than eleven teeth extracted!

George Christie had also picked up a nasty shoulder injury early on when he was brought down heavily and when he went into the dressing room at half time, he was suffering severe pain. The Dens Park doctor had to give him two pain killing injections and strap up the shoulder and at full time diagnosed the trouble as a pulled muscle in the shoulder.

Despite the pain, Christie nearly opened the scoring thirteen minutes after the break with a raking thirty yarder which was fisted onto the bar but it was a rare Dundee attack. The second half started where the first half ended with a string of Kilmarnock attacks and they very nearly took the lead on the hour when Gordon Frew had to make a last minute tackle when Henaughan was poised for a shot.

The tackle of Frew's, timed to a nicety was typical of the Dark Blues' defensive play throughout the match. From goal to left-half Dundee were magnificent but the problem was that wing halves Ziesing and Cowie had to concentrate on defence as The Dee struggled to mount an attack. Bobby Henderson also had to be at full stretch to deflect a Mays header wide and it looked a matter of time before Kilmarnock scored.

The turning point came however with just ten minutes left when Jimmy Toner went to his skipper Alfie Boyd and asked him if he could switch inside and when Boyd agreed he swapped places with Bert Henderson.

Two minutes later Toner got the ball from a midfield mix-up, feinted to make out to Henderson on the touchline and with the Killie defence on the wrong foot, put a peach of a pass through to Bobby Flavell. It was the first effective Dundee pass of the game and the first chance that Flavell had and he showed his appreciation by firing low past Niven to give Dundee a scarcely deserved lead.

It was Dundee 1 Kilmarnock 0 with just eight minutes left and on eighty-seven minutes, the Dark Blues doubled their lead and made certain that the cup was coming to Dens for the second year in a row. Bobby Henderson's long punt reached the Killie penalty box and as centre-half Thyne hesitated, Bobby Flavell rushed in. The wee centre let the ball bounce twice before racing in to thump the ball into the corner of the net in exactly the same spot as five minutes before.

In the dressing room Bobby Henderson said he couldn't get over the second goal and that he'd often kicked out the ball in the same fashion in ordinary games to no avail. However he'd done it when it counted most and his assist helped secure the 2-0 win the lift the cup.

Dundee had become the first side in the competition's history to retain the trophy and created the record that George Anderson had craved. The manager had followed the match at home with regular fifteen minute phone calls from Hampden in the first half and on the wireless in the second half and *The Courier* on Monday printed a photograph a delighted George Anderson with a beaming smile and his bowler hat on, sitting in his house next to his radio.

According to *The Sporting Post's* summary, *"The League Cup goes back to Dundee but they will never have to fight harder for a trophy. They have the opportunism of Bobby Flavell to thanks. Those two late goals were masterpieces of quick thinking."*

Trainer Reggie Smith summed it up by saying, *"One of the worst games we've played this season – but we won the cup."*

Doug Cowie agreed Dundee were lucky and in *Up Wi' The Bonnets: The Centenary History of Dundee* told author Norrie Price, *"I'll admit we were a wee bit lucky. We took a long time to get into our stride but at the end of the day it's goals that count and it was us who got them!"*

Lucky or not captain Alfie Boyd received the trophy from the Scottish League president on Dundee's behalf and was lifted shoulder on the pitch by his team mates. There were joyous scenes amongst the players and fans but the celebrations on the Hampden pitch were curtailed slightly after the heavens opened at the final whistle. The Kilmarnock crowd dispersed quickly in the rain but over 10,000 Dundonians milked it for all it was worth.

Telegrams of congratulations began to arrive from all over Scotland, England, America and various parts of the world including one from 'Four Staunch Supporters in Calcutta' saying *"It's Up Wi' the Topees of Bonnie Dundee!!"*

George Anderson had received one at home before the match from S.F.A. secretary Sir George Graham who said he regretted not being able to meet at Hampden as he was also recovering at home having taken ill at the Wales game in Cardiff the week before and also sent another congratulatory one at full time.

After drinking copious amounts of champagne from the cup in the dressing room, the Dundee party headed to Buchanan Street station to be greeted by a mass of Dark Blue and a huge cheer and Alfie Boyd showed the trophy off to the Dundee fans out of the window of the train as he had done the previous year. *The Sporting Post* announced that Dundee would be returning to Dundee West at 8.30pm and a jubilant crowd of 25,000 were booking their vantage points two hours before their arrival.

The train arrived five minutes late and when the Dark Blues stepped onto the platform they were greeted by Lord Provost William Black and his granddaughter and M.P. for Dundee East Morgan Thomson and his wife before being hustled out to their bus on Yeaman Shore via a side entrance.

It wasn't an open topped bus that greeted the players so they climbed up onto the roof to take the acclaim of their adoring public. George Christie was still in great pain and struggled to hoist himself onto the roof but once they were all on, Alfie Boyd held the cup aloft to a tumultuous cheer. The bus moved off at a snail's pace and as it wound its way through Whitehall Cresent and Whitehall Street into High Street, the crowds were lined up ten deep with trams and motor cars brought to a standstill.

A large crowd had assembled in the City Square, where the bus had done a circuit twelve months before but they were disappointed when the bus went up Reform Street and straight down to West Ferry by Victoria Road. They were heading to chairman James Gellaty's house in Albany Road for a club celebration and the crowd in the city centre dispersed quickly when they heard of the coach's destination.

At the celebration, Mr. Gellatly gave a toast and said, *"On behalf of the directors I want to thank all the players for this great achievement and I also thank those who prepared you for the game – Reggie Smith, Rueben Bennett and Harry Easson. You have all done a magnificent job. It is difficult to win the cup the first time but much more difficult to repeat the performance. I am sure Dundee is proud of you."*

From the chairman's house the party went on to the Royal British Hotel at 10pm for a victory dinner and a crowd of around 1500 converged to acclaim their heroes. It was chaos around the entrance and the players struggled to get in and when the crowd refused to budge, Bobby Flavell made a personal appeal from one of the windows. The crowd eventually moved but not before a sing song as their celebrations went on long into the night.

One of the guests of the official party was Mr. Ebbe Schwartz, president of the Denmark F.A. and he was impressed by the crowds he saw. *"This crowd of people is amazing"* he told Colin Glen of *The Courier. "Surely Dundee must have a population of a million people as I have never seen anything like this."*

Schwartz was a friend of Anderson and was over in Scotland to attend both the cup final and the wedding of Anderson's daughter the following Wednesday but unfortunately the wedding was postponed when Mrs. Anderson took ill. The day after the cup final she had to be removed to an Aberdeen nursing home suffering from a gastric ulcer and was confined to bed for several days.

Anderson had accompanied his wife in the ambulance and to the nursing home and when their daughter Mildred heard her mother had taken ill, she immediately postponed her big day. She didn't want to go through with it without her mother being present and Anderson therefore wired the 200 guests to let them know.

Mrs. Anderson was home by the end of the week and she was back in time for the visit of Dundee trainer Reggie Smith who had brought the League Cup to show his boss. Anderson was delighted to have the trophy on his sideboard for an afternoon and asked Smith tongue in cheek if he could suggest to the chairman that it should stay with him when he returned to Dens.

Anderson knew however that it belonged in the board room as a testament to the fantastic team effort that brought the cup back to Dens. He gave Smith a message to tell the players how proud he was of them and how proud he was that they had created history, not just in Dundee terms but in Scottish Football terms.

For a club like Dundee to become the first club to win the League Cup back to back was a phenomenal achievement and the players had earned themselves legendary status in the annals of Dark Blue history.

Chapter 28:
Gordon Frew

GORDON FREW WAS a polished and popular full-back who played for Dundee at both right-back and left-back for four years from 1950 to 1954, winning the Scottish League Cup with The Dark Blues in 1952.

Born in South Africa in 1927, Frew started his football career just after the Second World War with amateur side Wanderers in the Transvaal League before moving to the Marist Brothers A.F.C. in Johannesburg in 1947. That same year, Gordon was chosen to play for the South African national team against a touring Clyde side and in June 1950 he won his first full cap when he lined up against Australia in Durban.

The Socceroos were on a two-month tour of South Africa in June and July and played a further three 'test' internationals against their hosts and Frew played in all four Australian games at left-half in which the Springboks won two and lost two.

Just after those games, Frew was approached by a Dundee F.C. representative with a view to moving to Scotland and joining The Dee and he was delighted to jump at the chance of his first professional contract. Frew had qualified as a chartered accountant while playing with the Marists and agreed to sign a part-time contract while also finding an accountancy job in Dundee, which the club were willing to help with.

He was registered therefore with the Scottish League on August 12th 1950 but had to wait six months for his debut when he came in to replace the injured Gerry Follon at right-back for the visit of Celtic at Dens. It was a debut of mixed emotions for Frew as he put through his own net but it didn't stop the Dark Blues recording a fine 3-1 win over The Bhoys.

Gerry Follon returned the following week for a Scottish Cup first round tie with Dundee United but after the 2-2 draw at Dens, Frew came back in for the replay at Tannadice which the Dark Blues won 1-0 thanks to a goal from Billy Steel.

At the start of his second season, Frew played in the opening game in Paisley against St Mirren in the League Cup and played at left-back instead of the injured Jack Cowan. Over the next four years, Gordon would pretty much be a squad player with The Dee, making just sixty-three appearances, and despite joining Dundee as a left-half, he played in all of those games at full-back.

Frew played in five of the six sectional ties of the 1951/52 League Cup and in both legs of the quarter-final against Falkirk but was unlucky to be dropped for the semi-final against Motherwell when Jack Cowan reclaimed the number three jersey. Frew had played in all but one of that season's games to date, including seven appearances in the League Cup, but after The Dee defeated Motherwell 5-1 at Ibrox in the semi, it was Cowan who lined up against Rangers in the final.

The following season however it was the reverse when Jack Cowan had played in every match en route to Dundee's second final but got injured the week before against Hearts at Dens. Frew therefore got a call at work the day before the big match to tell him he was playing and was told to report at

Dundee West train station at 2.30pm with his boots being brought down for him from Dens Park.

Frew had played in three of the sectional ties at the start of the season but now lined up in the final against Kilmarnock at left-back. He played well, crucially kicking one off the line on the hour when it was still 0-0 and, after Bobby Flavell claimed a brace in the last eight minutes, Gordon won the first winner's medal of his career.

At the end of the season Frew travelled with the Dundee squad for their two-month, seventeen-match tour of homeland South Africa and played in all three tests against their national side.

In October, the South Africans visited Dundee as part of their tour of the British Isles and played in a friendly at Dens and Frew was made captain for the night. It was the first time Gordon had skippered the Dark Blues and two goals from Albert Henderson and one from Gerry Burrell made it a proud night for the South African with a 3-1 win against his country.

That season the 5ft 8in Frew made twenty-eight appearances for Dundee as he finally established himself in the team, but on February 20th 1954, he was part of the side which was on the wrong end of a shock when they were knocked out of the Scottish Cup 3-0 by 'C' Division Berwick Rangers at Shielfield.

It proved to be Gordon's last game for Dundee as, just a few days later, he announced that he wanted to return to South Africa alongside fellow countryman Ken Ziesing. Bobby Flavell also announced that he was keen to try his luck in South Africa, while Canadian Jack Cowan stated he also wanted to return home. Manager George Anderson said that the 'rebel four' would not play for Dundee again.

Frew therefore returned to South Africa in the summer and signed once again for the amateur Marist Brothers. Dundee retained his registration for another five years until April 1959, meaning that he was unable to sign for another professional side but was able to turn out for the Marists in the amateur Transvaal League where he joined Alfie Boyd who was coach.

It didn't stop Frew turning out for his country however and after a five year international hiatus while playing in Scotland, he was called up for the Springboks' tour of Australia in September 1955. Gordon was chosen to be captain for the trip and played in all four tests against the Socceroos and returned to his pre-Dundee position of left-half.

The following year he captained his country again in two matches against England in June 1956 as the F.A. toured South Africa and played this time at right-back as England won the games 4–3 and 4–2.

In 1959, the first professional league in South Africa, the National Football League, was formed and Frew was invited to become player/manager of the newly formed Highlands Park F.C. Dundee released Frew's registration to allow him to sign for Highlands Park and it was his job to put together a side to compete in the second N.F.L. season, having missed out on starting in its first.

It turned out to be a successful debut season for the new club as Frew led Highlands Park to the N.F.L. league championship and in their second year they won the Castle Cup, the national South African cup.

In their third year they won the league championship for the second time and at the end of the season Gordon decide to hang up his boots at the age of thirty-five. He decided to retire from the game altogether and resigned as manager to instead concentrate on his accountancy career. He had left a fine legacy at Balfour Park as Highlands Park would go on to win the championship six times in the next fifteen years including the title in 1975 with a certain Alan Gilzean in their ranks.

Gordon Frew always spoke highly of his time in Scotland and enjoyed his time at Dens and loved to tell stories of his time playing alongside Billy Steel & Co. as one of Dundee's Hampden Heroes.

Honours at Dundee:
Scottish League Cup winners: 1952/53

Appearances:

League:	44
Scottish Cup:	5
League Cup:	13
Other:	1
Total:	63

Chapter 29:
Four In A Row?

THE WEEK AFTER the League Cup victory over Kilmarnock, Dundee slumped to an embarrassing 3-2 defeat against East Fife at Bayview and the following week wasn't much better with a tedious 0-0 draw with St Mirren at Dens. The 16,500 crowd had been in good spirits before the match with the League Cup trophy being piped round the pitch for the second year in a row by the Dundee Cadet Band but they were leaving well before the end of a turgid match.

The St Mirren match was the first of four games where Dundee failed to score but more worryingly, that defeat in Methil signalled an astonishing four-month slump where the Dark Blues won just two league games in seventeen matches. By the end of February, they lay next to the foot of the table but a 2-0 win over defending champions Hibernian on March 7th sparked a mini revival which saw George Anderson's men eventually finish seventh, just one point behind fourth.

Rangers would win the 'A' Division with just forty-three points, finishing ahead of Hibs on goal average. It was the lowest points total to win the Championship since 1905 when there were only fourteen teams in the league and twenty-six games played and if Dundee hadn't gone on such a bad run, they could have been in the mix. The Dark Blues finished with twenty-nine points and if they managed to transform their eleven draws into wins or win half of the games they lost, they could have unfurled their first league flag.

By Christmas it became obvious therefore than any further glory that season would have to come in the Scottish Cup, where Dundee would be aiming to reach their another Hampden cup final. Could they make it four in a row?

Two days after winning the League Cup *The Evening Telegraph* was already looking forward to the Scottish Cup which was still three months away as in its editorial it said, '*The Dark Blues have a chance of pulling off a League Cup and Scottish Cup double. They failed at the last hurdle last season to accomplish this feat which has never been achieved before.*'

The first round of the sixty-eighth Scottish Cup with all Scottish League teams entered was due to be played on January 24th 1953 but Dundee were fortunate enough to get a bye. With no game at the weekend, Dundee travelled down to Hull City in midweek to keep the players match fit and did their confidence no harm at all with a 4-1 win thanks to goals from Toner, Steel and Flavell (2).

It was good to have Steel back as he had missed the last two league games through injury. Steel wasn't the only one who had been injured in recent weeks as Follon, Ziesing, Flavell and Hill had all missed games in recent weeks which no doubt contributed to Dundee's poor form.

When the second round draw was made on January 26th, the Dark Blues couldn't have got it any tougher as they were drawn at home to league leaders Rangers. The Ibrox side were unbeaten in fourteen matches and as soon as the draw was made, Dundee announced the game would be all-ticket.

Such was the interest in the tie that the Dens Park record crowd was smashed for the third year in a row with a staggering 43,024 inside the fifty-four-year-old ground. It is a record that still stands today, having never been bettered since – not even in the fabulous European Cup run ten years later – and with the current capacity sitting at 11,856, it is a record that will never be broken.

Football attendances enjoyed a post-war boom and Dundee F.C. were no different. Dens Park's top four record attendances all came in the eight years after the Second World War, while the highest attendance to watch Dundee in any match was the 136,990 who at the 1952 Scottish Cup Final at Hampden. The Scottish Cup traditionally enjoyed bigger crowds that league matches and seven of Dens Park's top ten crowds have been for Scottish Cup ties.

	Date	Attendance	Opponents	Competition
1.	7 February 1953	43,024	Rangers	Scottish Cup
2.	18 February 1956	42,500	Rangers	Scottish Cup
3.	8 March 1952	41,000	Aberdeen	Scottish Cup (QF)
4.	10 March 1951	40,920	Raith Rovers	Scottish Cup (QF)
5.	12 March 1963	40,000	Anderlecht	European Cup (QF)
6.	3 January 1949	39,975	Rangers	League
7.	12 September 1947	39,000	Rangers	League Cup (Sectional)
8	14 February 1931	38,099	Aberdeen	Scottish Cup
9.	28 March 1947	38,000	Aberdeen	Scottish Cup (QF)
10.	27 January 1951	38,000	Dundee United	Scottish Cup

The match itself ended in disappointment as a 2-0 Rangers win ended Dundee's chances of a double, double cup final appearance at the first hurdle.

Dundee played some neat football but with little penetration up front, they rarely looked like winning. It was two blunders within sixty seconds which gave Rangers their victory and it was a desperately disappointing way to be knocked out of the cup. The first came from Bill Brown who was back in goal for the second match in a row as he was home on leave but he misjudged the ball to allow Hubbard to give the Light Blues the lead. The second blunder came from Gerry Follon almost from the restart when he allowed Gierson to nip in to make it 2-0 and there was no way back for the Dark Blues.

The £3,270 gate receipts brought a measure of consolation but with two months of the season remaining, Dundee's season was effectively over.

The last home game on April 4th was a satisfying 4-0 win over Celtic with goals from Flavell, Toner and two from Albert Henderson and after the match the players had to go to the boardroom to be presented with their League Cup winners medals from chairman James Gellatly.

George Anderson was able to put his on the wooden plaque he was given by a Hearts director, Bobby Flavell, whose goals had won the cup, got his made into a chain for his daughter as promised, while Ken Ziesing posted his home to his parents in South Africa.

Despite a fairly disappointing league season, there was no disguising the fact that the season had been a major success with the club winning only the third trophy in its history. Mr. Gellatly spoke of how proud he was of the players for achieving the feat of becoming the first team to retain the League Cup and making the city very proud once again.

It was a marvellous achievement from a wonderful team who had well and truly written their name into Dens Park folklore and deserved the acclaim.

Chapter 30:
Ken Ziesing

WHEN GEORGE ANDERSON was trying to build his cosmopolitan side of the early Fifties, he invited half a dozen South African players to come over to Dens and one of those, Ken Ziesing, was an undoubted success. Only two of the South African players actually made the Dark Blues first team and alongside Gordon Frew, Ziesing won a League Cup winner's medal in 1952.

Born in Johannesburg in 1926, Ziesing joined the Marist Brothers A.F.C. in 1946 when they reformed after the war and twelve months later he won his first representative honour when he was selected up to play for South Africa against Clyde when they were touring the Dominion.

In 1950, Ziesing was called up to the South African squad to face the touring Australians but, unfortunately, wasn't selected to play in any of the four tests. In was during his time with the Springboks however that he was approached by an agent for Dundee F.C. and in the summer of 1950, he flew over to Scotland to sign for The Dark Blues.

Ziesing signed for Dundee on August 12th 1950 but had to wait until January 2nd 1951 before he made his debut against Morton at Dens. Ken made an instant impact by scoring on his debut and in his next two games he netted against Falkirk and Celtic to make it three goals in three games.

Ziesing played in those games as the centre-forward at number nine where he had played for the Marist Brothers but in the coming months he was to be transformed into one of the classiest right-halves in Scotland. His ground passing was immaculate and his head flicks were of great value and he was adept at turning defence into attack.

Ziesing's change in position was due to the signing of the potent centre-forward Bobby Flavell but Ken was still worth a goal or two to the team. In the second game of the 1951/52 season, Ziesing scored a brace in a 2-1 sectional League Cup win against Hearts at Dens and scored again in the return at Tynecastle and in the quarter-final against Falkirk scored the opener in a hard fought 2-1 victory.

By the time the semi-final came around, Ziesing had dropped out of the side with George Hill returning from injury and he was unable to regain his place by the time of the final in October. He did however travel to Hampden as the reserve and was delighted when the Dark Blues won and was on the pitch at the end to celebrate with his team mates. Ken can be seen in the photographs looking immaculate in his club tie and blazer as Alfie Boyd is lifted onto the shoulders of Tommy Gallacher and Billy Steel with the trophy.

By the end of his debut season, the 6ft 1in Ziesing had scored eight goals in twenty appearances and he was popular with both his team mates and fans. He had been unfortunate to have repeated trouble with pulled muscles which had restricted his number of appearances but after a good pre-season, declared himself, *"As fit as a fiddle."*

Ziesing started the 1952/53 season at right-half in the number four jersey and was keeping Tommy Gallacher out of the side. Gallacher had been part of the legendary half-back line of Gallacher,

Cowie and Boyd but with Cowie and Boyd switching places and Ziesing coming in for Tommy after the public trial game, it was a new half-back line that started the defence of the League Cup.

Ken played in all six sectional game and in both legs of the quarter-final against Stirling Albion and, in the semi-final against Hibs at Tynecastle, he put in a fantastic performance which *The Sporting Post* described as, *'Ziesing's best performance in a dark blue shirt in a country mile which more than helped Dundee to Hampden.'*

Dundee defeated Hibernian 2-1 in a magnificent match and now Ken could look forward to the final. Having been on the pitch at the end of the final twelve months ago, he was now on it for real when The Dark Blues lined up against Kilmarnock.

Killie attacked Dundee from the off and it took a sterling rearguard performance, in which Ziesing was at the heart, to keep the Ayrshire part-timers at bay. Two late goals by Bobby Flavell however sealed the win as Dundee took the League Cup back to Tayside for the second year in succession.

Ken was delighted with the win, the first major victory in his career, and when he got his hands on his medal towards the end of the season, he immediately despatched it back to South Africa to his proud parents.

Ziesing wasn't far behind his medal however as he was part of Dundee's squad to tour his homeland for two months from May to July 1953. Dundee played a gruelling seventeen-game schedule which included three matches against the South African national side and Ziesing played in all three of the 'tests' against his countrymen.

The following October South Africa came to Scotland on their British tour and played Dundee in a friendly at Dens. Ziesing impressed the visiting South African officials and they asked if he would consider returning to the Dominion so that he could turn out regularly for the Springboks himself.

In February 1954 therefore, in the wake of an embarrassing Scottish Cup defeat to 'C' Division Berwick, Ziesing told George Anderson of his intention to return home. When Gordon Frew, Jack Cowan and Bobby Flavell also expressed an intention to leave Dens Park, Anderson labelled them the 'rebel four' and said they would never play for Dundee again.

It was a sad end to his Dark Blue career and in the summer he returned to his old club in Johannesburg, the Marist Brothers, as an amateur because Dundee refused to release his registration and held onto it until 1959. In his first year back he won the Transvaal League championship alongside Gordon Frew and won the Transvaal Challenge Cup in four out of the next six seasons, scoring in the 1957 final victory over Benoni F.C.

Almost immediately upon returning, Ziesing was called up by the South African national team and played in all five matches for the Springboks when they toured Australia in September 1955. He felt it justified his move back home having not been called by his country during his four years at Dens.

He did however win a League Cup medal at Dens which he claimed was the highlight of his career when he retired in 1962 and in the same year, he sent a telegram to Dens Park congratulating them on becoming Champions of Scotland. *"Dundee Football Club, the city and people are never very far from my heart,"* he said.

Honours at Dundee:
Scottish League Cup winners: 1952/53

Appearances, Goals:

League:	45, 7 goals
Scottish Cup:	6, 1 goal
League Cup:	23, 5 goals
Other:	1
Totals:	75, 13 goals

Chapter 31:
Tartan Troops From Tayside

AT THE END of the season, Dundee were snubbed by the football authorities who declined to invite the Dark Blues to participate in the Coronation Cup to celebrate the accession of Queen Elizabeth II. Four clubs from England – Arsenal, Manchester United, Newcastle United and Tottenham Hotspur, were joined by four from Scotland – Celtic, Rangers, Aberdeen and Hibernian. Rangers had won the League and Scottish Cups while Aberdeen and Hibs were invited as runners-up in both. Dundee felt aggrieved as they had won back to back League Cups and finished higher in the League than both Celtic and Aberdeen but in the event, the tournament was won by Celtic

Instead of taking the huff, Dundee contented themselves with a summer tour of South Africa, organised by the flamboyant Anderson as part of the club's sixtieth anniversary celebrations. The tour also however assisted the S.F.A., which found itself unable to fulfil a commitment it had already made. Considering their snub received in the Coronation Cup fiasco, it was a conciliatory gesture by Anderson but he was always a master of both diplomacy and publicity.

Dundee flew out to South Africa therefore a fortnight after their last game of the season away to league champions Rangers. Dundee took a sixteen-man squad with them and along with manager George Anderson and the directors, flew direct from London to Johannesburg on a BOAC Comet.

After their League Cup successes, the Dundee squad were now well known sporting figures and they were able to trade on their name in the Dominion by appearing in adverts and doing promotional work which helped enhance their bonuses.

The tour was coordinated by George Anderson's friend and Dundonian Haldane Stewart, who would later manage Morton and they stayed in the best of hotels wherever they went. They were based in Johannesburg where each player had a room to themselves although when Anderson saw the room that seventeen-year-old Dave Easson had, with a wonderful view of the beach, he immediately made the youngster swap as he only had a view of the service entrance at the rear.

Dundee's first match took place against Southern Transvaal in Johannesburg on May 16th 1953 and when they took to the field in front of 22,000, they were wearing not their regular dark blue but rather an Anderson tartan strip with a Dundee badge on the left breast chosen by manager George Anderson.

Anderson was well aware of the benefits of good publicity and as the side started to get changed for their first match, he came into the dressing room with a parcel with their new strips stating, *"These will take a trick out there."* When they took to the field, the new shirts were given a great reception by the local fans and the following day, the newspaper headlines read, *'Tartan Troops From Tayside'*, as they reported on the 1-1 draw.

Bobby Flavell, who had finished the trophy winning season with twenty-five goals, got Dundee's strike against Southern Transvaal and in their second game against Natal in Pietermarizburg, he scored a hat-trick with 'Pud' Hill getting Dundee's other counter in a 4-1 win.

Three days later in Durban, Dundee went one better, winning 5-0 in a rematch with Natal and Flavell was again on the mark with a double with Billy Steel, Doug Cowie and Alfie Boyd from the penalty spot completing the scoring.

Dundee were greeted very warmly everywhere they went and with a large number of Scottish ex-pats in South Africa, they enjoyed scores of functions and receptions by Caledonian societies.

The players were given their match fees immediately after every game, even if they didn't play, to help them enjoy the trip as much as possible. For one trip away from Johannesburg, Albert Henderson had to remain behind as he had fallen ill and Dave Easson also had to stay to look after him, but as soon as the Dundee party returned, George Anderson went straight up to see how they were doing before he went to his own room and gave them their wages for the match, despite the fact they didn't even travel.

Dundee repeated their 5-0 scoreline in their fourth game on May 27th against a Border XI in East London with Ronnie Turnbull, who had just returned to the club from Swansea after spells with Sunderland and Manchester City, scoring twice alongside the fit again Bert Henderson, Billy Steel with a penalty and Doug Cowie who had now scored the same of goals on tour as his entire seven-year Dundee career.

Dundee's free-scoring form continued with a 5-0 win over Eastern Province in Port Elizabeth and a 4-0 win over Western Province in Cape Town, and with the Dundee party moving to a different location for every match in their first month in South Africa, they were getting a fantastic opportunity to experience and visit the whole country.

Dundee were on their travels again as they defeated Griqualand 2-0 in the Northern Cape in Kimberley, Eastern Transvaal 4-2 in Benoni before an impressive 9-2 rout over Orange Free State in 2010 World Cup venue Bloemfontein, in which Ronnie Turnbull scored a hat-trick.

On June 14th they faced a Lourenco Marques XI 3-1 in Port East Africa and a brace from Cowie and one from Flavell earned a 3-1 win. Lourenco Marques was the capital of Mozambique before it gained independence from Portugal in 1975 and is today known as Maputo and the representative side they sent across the border to face Dundee was a mixture of African and Portuguese players.

Dundee's next two matches were also at 2010 venues with a 2-0 win over Northern Transvaal in Pretoria and a 4-0 win in the second game against Southern Transvaal in Johannesburg. The South Transvaal match was unusual in that in front of a crowd of 10,000 it was played under floodlights, which was an innovation that was still in its infancy. After some unsuccessful experiments with floodlights in the late nineteenth century, the first match in Scotland played under 'proper' floodlights was in November 1951 in a friendly between Stenhousemuir and Hibs and they weren't used in competitive games until 1956, so it would have been a unique experience for the Dundee players.

All these matches however were warm-ups for the three-game test series against the South African national team and the first of these came in Durban on June 27th when Dundee suffered their first defeat of their tour when South Africa won 1-0.

Dundee however bounced back in their next two matches in a double header against Southern Rhodesia with a 4-1 win in Salisbury in which Doug Cowie scored a hat-trick and an 8-0 victory in Bulawayo.

The second test match against South Africa took place in Johannesburg on July 11th and when they arrived at the stadium, they discovered that there were no shorts with the kit when unpacking the hamper. Reggie Smith had been responsible for the kit and in trying to hide the tartan shirts, had forgotten to pack the team's shorts for the match.

When Smith told the South African team manager Mr. M. Shackleton, he organised a police car and convoy to take Dave Easson back to the team hotel to collect the shorts. They travelled through the streets in Johannesburg with all the lights set at green with a police motorcade and when Easson returned with the shorts just twenty minutes later much to Smith's relief, he couldn't believe what their South African hosts did in an effort to help them out.

Tartan shirts and recovered shorts on, Dundee were led on to the field by a pipe band and they gained revenge for that earlier loss with an emphatic 5-0 win. Bobby Flavell scored his second hat-trick of the tour in the Rand Stadium and the other two goals were scored by Ronnie Turnbull and Dundee's very own South African, Ken Ziesing.

Four days later in Cape Town, Zeising was again on the score sheet as Dundee played the last of their seventeen matches and won the third test against South Africa 5-3. Additional goals from Steel, Cowie and a Turnbull double meant Dundee won the test series against their hosts by two matches to one and it was a very enjoyable end to a memorable trip.

The two-month trip was a marvellous experience for the Dundee players and officials as they won fifteen of their games with one win and a draw and scored an impressive seventy goals, conceding twelve. Bobby Flavell would finish top scorer with seventeen goals with Ronnie Turnbull in second, scoring twelve while Doug Cowie went home with nine goals to boast about, having only scored twice in competitive games for Dundee since 1946.

The results of Dundee's South African tour were as follows:

DATE	VENUE	OPPOSITION	SCORE	SCORERS
16/ 05/1953	Johannesburg	Southern Transvaal	1-1	Flavell
20/05/1953	Pietermarizburg	Natal	4-1	Flavell (3), Hill
23/05/1953	Durban	Natal	5-0	Flavell (2), Steel, Cowie, Boyd (pen)
27/05/1953	East London	Border XI	5-0	Turnbull (2), Cowie Henderson, Steel (pen)
30/05/1953	Port Elizabeth	Eastern Province	5-0	Easson (2), Christie Turnbull (2)
06/06/1953	Capetown	Western Province	4-0	Flavell, Turnbull, Henderson (2)
10/06/1953	Kimberley	Griqualand	2-0	Christie, Flavell
13/06/1953	Benoni	Eastern Transvaal	4-2	Steel, Flavell (2), Christie
14/06/1953	Port East Africa	Lourenco Marques XI	3-1	Flavell, Cowie (2)
17/06/1953	Bloemfontein	Orange Free State	9-2	Turnbull (3), Flavell, Christie (2), Steel (2), Walker
20/06/1953	Pretoria	Northern Transvaal	2-0	Hill, Henderson
23/06/1953	Johannesburg	Southern Transvaal	4-0	Steel, Ziesing, Christie (2)
27/06/1953	Durban	South Africa	0-1	
01/07/1953	Salisbury	Southern Rhodesia	4-1	Cowie (3), Hill
04/07/1953	Bulawayo	Southern Rhodesia	8-0	Christie (2), Cowan, Flavell (2), Turnbull, Cowie, Steel
11/07/1953	Johannesburg	South Africa	5-0	Flavell (3), Turnbull, Ziesing
15/07/1953	Cape Town	South Africa	5-3	Turnbull (2), Cowie, Steel, Ziesing

Dundee played in six of the nine cities which hosted the 2010 World Cup matches and at the end of the trip, captain Alfie Boyd decided he would stay in South Africa having been offered a coaching post with the Marist Brothers club.

It meant that Boyd missed the return game with South Africa when they visited Dens Park in October as part of their two-month tour of the British Isles and Europe and the match ended in a 3–1 Dundee win, with goals from Albert Henderson (2) and Gerry Burrell.

South African football was very much in development at this time and they were one of only four African nations to attend F.I.F.A.'s 1953 congress and demanded, and won, African representation on the F.I.F.A. executive committee. Fifty-seven years later, South Africa hosted their own World Cup and football had progressed a long way from the time when the 'Tartan Troops from Tayside' had toured their country.

Chapter 32:
Albert Henderson

ALBERT HENDERSON WAS signed from juvenile club Aberdeen Lads Club on November 24th 1951 and within a year, the twenty-year-old was one of Dundee's Hampden Heroes when he played in the 1952 Scottish League Cup Final win over Kilmarnock.

One of a number of Aberdonians signed by manager George Anderson from his home town, Albert Henderson was a 5ft 10in inside-forward and his signature was won from under the noses of a number of English clubs who were chasing his services. During his National Service with the Army he won five medals and played in many representative matches and his signing was seen as something of a coup by the Dens Park side.

Bert didn't have wait very long for his first team debut as less than a month after joining he played against Stirling Albion at Dens on December 22nd and he was an instant hero by scoring in the 4-1 win. Three days later he retained his place against Partick Thistle at Firhill on Christmas Day and gave the Dark Blues fans the perfect gift with another goal in a 3-1 victory.

By the end of his first professional season, Henderson had made eleven appearances, scoring eight times and, as well as making full use of his height in a short forward line, his bursts of speed and fine positional play were an asset to the side. He didn't play in the Scottish Cup Final against Motherwell in April, with the experienced Johnny Pattillo being preferred at inside-right, but in truth Albert hadn't been expecting to play as he hadn't featured in the previous four games.

He did however come in for the last game of the season against Third Lanark at Dens the following week and signed off a promising debut season with a brace in a 6-0 win.

Bert had also played his part in the Dundee 'A' side winning the Scottish League 'C' Division 1951/52 title with eighteen appearances and the start of the following season saw Bert begin in the reserves. However, after a number of impressive performances, he was called into the first team in time for the League Cup quarter-final against Stirling Albion and played in both legs.

He was trading places with Tommy Gallacher over the next few weeks after Tommy had been moved up to inside-right at the start of the season but it was Henderson who was given the number eight jersey in the 2-1 League Cup semi-final win over Hibs at Tynecastle.

In the two 'A' Division games between the semi and final, Henderson was on the scoresheet and so, on October 25th 1952, Bert was chosen ahead of Gallacher for the League Cup Final against Kilmarnock at Hampden.

The twenty-one-year-old however was a bag of nerves and put in a shaky performance and with the game still goalless with ten minutes to go, Jimmy Toner suggested that they should swap places and that Bert should go out on to the wing. It was a move that worked instantly as, just a few minutes later, Toner played Bobby Flavell through from the inside-right position and the centre fired low into the net to give Dundee the lead.

Henderson looked better on the touchline and made a couple of penetrating runs late on and when

Bobby Flavell got his second with just three minutes left, Albert's winner's medal was assured.

Henderson played twenty-six times, scoring six goals that year and at the end of the season was chosen for Dundee's sixteen-man squad to travel to South Africa for a two-month, seventeen-game tour. He spent a couple of days in bed in his hotel room with a stomach complaint which caused him to miss one of the games but he came back from the Dominion having scored four times in ten appearances.

Henderson also scored a brace against South Africa when they visited Dens in October 1953 and that season saw him score a total of nine goals in competitive games including the winner against Rangers at Dens in a 1-0 win.

In season 1954/55 Bert recorded his best tallies for Dundee in both goals and appearances when he scored ten times in thirty-seven appearances, the second best turn out of the squad.

In February 1956, Henderson scored in another notable game when he netted against Dundee United in a Scottish Cup fifth round tie. The sides hadn't met for five years and so there was great local interest in the match and, after a 2-2 draw at Tannadice, Dundee knocked the 'B' Division side out with a 3-0 win at Dens, with Henderson scoring the third.

In December 1957, Henderson submitted a transfer request after a delay in receiving a £1,000 benefit and Dundee manager Willie Thornton then dropped him for the next game against Falkirk. Dundee claimed that they had asked the Scottish League's permission and it was their delay in responding that was the problem and that Henderson therefore had no right to put in a transfer request. He subsequently withdrew it and went on to play for the Dark Blues for another three years.

In January 1961, St. Mirren sold Johnny Frye to Sheffield Wednesday for £3,500 and the Paisley side immediately spent £2,500 of the cash on buying Albert Henderson from Dundee on January 13th. Dundee manager Bob Shankly then used that money to sign Bobby Wishart from Aberdeen for £3,500 and Wishart would go on to score two goals on his debut against Dundee United the following week and would be a key member of Dundee's league championship winning team eighteen months later.

Henderson left Dundee aged thirty after nine years at Dens and was the club's second longest serving player behind Doug Cowie. He played 271 times for the Dark Blues, scoring over fifty goals, including a hat-trick against Arbroath in the Forfarshire Cup shortly before he left, a club he would soon be managing.

Within a year at Love Street, a knee injury prematurely ended Bert's playing career and at the age of thirty-one he was invited to become manager of Arbroath. He would be in charge at Gayfield for the next eighteen years, becoming the longest serving manager in Scotland at that time and he oversaw arguably the best period of the Red Lichties' history.

In the thirteen years up to the creation of the Premier League in 1975, Arbroath were promoted twice and spent a total of four seasons in Scotland's top division. Even away from the top flight, the Lichties under Henderson were always challenging for promotion, were third on three occasions and never finished lower than seventh in the old Second Division. His eye for quality also led to Gayfield being graced by players like Gordon Marshall, Andy Penman, Hugh Robertson, Ernie Winchester, Cammy Murray and Jimmy Bone who, although all nearing the end of their playing careers, still had the qualities Bert recognised as being vital in a balanced team. Others who starred in his sides included Billy Pirie, Tommy Walker and John Fletcher—the last-named having scored a late winning goal when Arbroath beat Rangers 3-2 at Ibrox in 1974. Heady days at Gayfield indeed!

Henderson, who used to collect gramophone records along with George Christie and was a great table tennis player, had been a valuable player for The Dee and always in the work-house of the team. Bobby Cox described him as, *"A hard player and a real team man – a great servant to the club."* and a compliment from man who embodies everything great about the Dark Blues is all you need to know about the youngest of Dundee's Hampden Heroes.

Honours at Dundee:
Scottish League Cup winners: 1952/53

Appearances, Goals:

League:	217, 47 goals
Scottish Cup:	10, 1 goal
League Cup:	44, 2 goals
Totals:	271, 50 goals

Chapter 33:
The End of an Era

POST-WAR DUNDEE WAS a vibrant city and Billy Steel & Co. were very much part of that vibrancy. By the mid 1950s however it was starting to change out of all recognition as modernisation began to transform the landscape, not only in the city centre but also in the north where new 'avenues of hope' housing schemes were being built while at the same time, the great Dundee side began to break up, marking the end of an era both on and off the park.

Dundee was, and is, and beautiful city, built around the rock of an extinct volcano known locally as The Law. When approaching the city by train across the longest rail bridge in Europe, the magnificence of Dundee can be glimpsed and the skyline of Alfie Boyd's Dundee had yet to be contaminated by the high rise flats or 'multis' built in the sixties. Dundonians returning home from the south often get goose bumps at the site of the city as it stretches along the River Tay's estuary from Broughty Ferry in the east to Invergowrie in the west.

Dundonians are fiercely proud of their heritage and while some observers have described it as 'dour, grey or dull', this couldn't be further from the truth for anyone who hails from, or has spent any time in the city. The view from The Law is spectacular; the promontory of Broughty Ferry, the green hills of Fife, the Sidlaws to the north, Balgay Hill to the west and the hinterland of Perthshire which can be spied across the Tay valley are amongst the views that give Dundee its flavour and the stories that exist within the visual feast are rich and warm.

There was also Lochee with its rich character – not yet defaced by the roadways and concrete blocks – and the famous Cox's Stack tower to the north-west, a testament to the importance of jute to Dundee. Then there was the Hilltown and the city centre to the south and to the north-east were Dens Park and Tannadice, home of the city's two football clubs, Dundee F.C. and Dundee United and the view of their grounds was vastly different to the one that exists today.

Dens and Tannadice are separated by a Bill Brown goal kick and sharing the same street, they are the two closest senior football grounds in the world. In 1952, Dens Park was an altogether different venue from the one today as there were no box-work all-seater stands. Dens was uncovered on three sides as the South Enclosure wasn't built until 1960 and the terracing bowl went round from the east side in front of the T.C. Keay factory, round to Dens Road on the south, to the west terracing on the Provost Road.

On the north side was the main grandstand which exists today with its unique v-shape to give spectators in the wing stands a better view. Designed by renowned football architect Archibald Leitch, it opened in 1921 and is a reminder today of a bygone era of players of a different age with their ankle length boots and replaceable leather studs.

Road transport in the 1950s was still on the whole poor. To travel to other Scottish cities could take the best part of a day as there were few by-passes and no motorways. For the keener Dundee football fan, travel to away games was mostly undertaken by train but with two football clubs in the city, fans of either persuasion would often watch Dundee one week and United the next. United were the poor relations in the early Fifties, languishing in the 'B' Division. As such, they often earned sympathetic support from Dundee fans on matchdays when the Dark Blues were playing away from home.

Within the city, tramcars were the main mode of transport and the city centre was a curious array of streets, particularly around the old Overgate. When the League Cup came to Dens for the first time, the old Wellgate still ran up from the end of the Murraygate to the bottom of the Hilltown and that would take you to Dens, provided you could negotiate the steep climb.

The corner of the now-vanished D.M. Brown on Commercial Street was a favourite meeting place for Dundonians and legend has it that Billy Steel was once found sitting on the pavement there by frantic Dundee F.C. staff, still drunk from the night before on the morning of a game. The story goes that he was taken up to Dens, given copious amounts of coffee and a cold shower and went out to score two goals.

The city of Dundee was built on jute and the city became known for its 'Three Js' – Jute, Jam and Journalism. By the beginning of the twentieth century there were 30,000 Dundonians working in Dundee's jute mills out of a population of 150,000. Jute gave Dundee its unique character and the smell of jute was in the air in the same way the smell from the breweries hung around the air in Edinburgh. The whiff of jute won't easily be forgotten by anyone who was brought up in the first half of the twentieth century.

Jute contributed to every aspect of life in Dundee, not least its dialect and it made the mill owners rich. Many built themselves mansions in either Broughty Ferry or in the west end near the Perth Road and over the years many of the jute barons invested their money in shares in Dundee Football Club and became directors on the board.

Jam and marmalade production at Keillors was another staple of Dundee life as was the publishing firm D.C. Thomson & Co. which produced such titles as *The Courier*, *The Sunday Post*, *The Dandy* and *The Beano*.

There was far less consumer spending in those days and in 1952 the average working wage was around £589 per annum. Luxuries were rare and even holidays for Dundonians were rarely taken further afield than Broughty Ferry.

Like any Scottish city, Dundee had its fair share of public houses, most of which closed at 10pm and stayed shut on Sundays. There were thirteen picture houses or cinemas in the city in 1950 but the most popular form of entertainment in the city was football. In the season Billy Steel signed for the Dark Blues, Dundee's average crowd at Dens Park was 23,500 and the club's record crowd was beaten three years in a row from 1951 to 1953.

It was amongst this background that George Anderson brought unprecedented success to Dundee with two League Cup wins, one Scottish Cup Final appearance and one Scottish League Championship runners-up spot in a three-year period. By the summer of 1954 however, Anderson was still dogged by the ill-health that caused him to miss the 1952 League Cup Final and he finally stepped down as manager, though retaining his seat on the board.

Many thought that assistant Reggie Smith was the logical successor but his replacement was veteran Rangers and Scotland centre-forward Willie Thornton, a somewhat surprising choice. Smith had been offered the post on a joint basis with Bobby Ancell back in 1949 but he turned it down, but now having gained coaching certificates both north and south of the border, he seemed the obvious successor to Anderson.

Smith was far from happy with Thornton's appointment and in September he set an example that was to be followed by Jim McLean in similar circumstances seventeen years later when he took the short walk down Tannadice Street to become manager of Dundee United.

Anderson's departure and Thornton's appointment signalled that the good times were coming to an end. Already Cowan, Frew and Ziesing had left and Jimmy Toner was given a free transfer. A number of the squad such as Follon, Gallacher, Hill and Flavell (who had decided to stay after being dropped as one of the 'Rebel Four') were in the twilight of their careers and it was apparent to Thornton that a major rebuilding task had to be undertaken.

Before Anderson left it had been discovered that Billy Steel had not been training as regularly at Firhill as was thought and in April Steel was given an ultimatum that he must train full time at Dens. Steel refused as he still had his sports shop in Glasgow and George Anderson put his superstar up for sale.

No offers were received for the thirty-one-year-old and three months later, after refusing new terms from Thornton, he shocked Scottish football once again by announcing his departure to the U.S.A. He was to become manager of the Los Angeles Danes and with a job, car and house thrown in, he would earn around $600 a month; four times his Dens Park salary!

It wasn't the last that Dundee heard of Billy Steel however as two years later Willie Thornton received a letter out of the blue from Steel. Things had not gone well for him in America as, after only six games, he was dropped by the L.A. Danes before a driving offence earned him adverse publicity that the club did not like. He moved to San Francisco where he did not play for eighteen months until he signed for Hollywood F.C. early in 1956.

Now the thirty-three-year-old wanted to return to Dundee, claiming he still had two years left in him and asked Willie Thornton for a trial. Thornton agreed to the request and was happy to welcome back a prodigal son but in true 'Budgem' style, nothing more was heard from him again.

To replace Reggie Smith, Willie Thornton brought in former Arsenal player Archie MacAuley as his right-hand man. MacAuley had played in the same Great Britain side as Billy Steel against the Rest of Europe in 1949 but his ideas of coaching and tactics were radically different to those that had been used under 'Toffee Dod'. Instead of an open attacking style, MacAuley wanted Dundee to defend deep, retreating to the eighteen-yard line when the opposition had the ball and these tactics became unpopular with established internationalists such as Doug Cowie.

Thornton was also keen to model his Dundee side on Rangers' defensive style of the time and although it served the Ibrox side well, the results at Dens did not come.

Thornton however was willing to give youth a chance and in the next few years he gave debuts to Pat Liney, Alex Hamilton, Bobby Cox, Ian Ure, Andy Penman, Alan Cousin, Alan Gilzean, Hugh Robertson and George McGeachie, who would all win the Scottish League Championship with Dundee.

His side was nicknamed the 'Thornton Babes' by some sections of the press and in April 1956 beat the 'Busby Babes' of Manchester United 5-1 – the game in which Bobby Charlton made his Manchester United debut – just after they had been crowned Champions of England.

As the youth came through, the old guard of the Anderson era were phased out and when Bob Shankly took over as manager in September 1959 only Doug Cowie and Bert Henderson remained from the League Cup winners. Henderson left Dundee in January 1961 when he was sold to St. Mirren and just six months later, Doug Cowie followed him out of Dens when Bob Shankly gave him a free transfer.

Cowie's release severed the last connection of the George Anderson golden years and it appeared to many that Shankly had purposefully rid the club of the last of the Anderson old boys. In the *Dundee Greats* book, Cowie said: *"Whether Bob saw me as the last of the Anderson men about the place and maybe felt I had too much influence I don't know. It was a blow."* Thirty-four-year-old Cowie was even more disappointed when Shankly signed Gordon Smith, a player three years a senior a few weeks later and his departure denied Cowie a league winner's medal when the Dark Blues became Champions of Scotland eight months later.

After ten years without any silverware Bob Shankly won the Scottish League Championship with a wonderful side and delivered the prize that George Anderson could not. Anderson however had built Dundee up after the war from a second division side to a Scottish football, trophy-winning force and started the legacy that Shankly was able to build upon. Without the vision and endeavour of George Anderson and his team, the Scottish League Championship might not have come to Dens. To that we should all doff our bowler hats to 'Toffee Dod'.

Chapter 34:
The Management

THERE IS LITTLE doubt that the post-war success enjoyed by Dundee F.C. had much to do with the management team of George Anderson, Reggie Smith and Reuben Bennett. All were former players with the Dark Blues and combined superbly to lead Dundee to glory and they were repeatedly praised by directors, players and fans alike.

George Anderson was the flamboyant managing-director with a penchant for publicity and he raised the profile of the Dark Blues immeasurably, leading them to their first silverware in over four decades. He liked to sit in the directors' box on a match day and just visited Dens a couple of times a week, the day to day running being left to Smith and Bennett.

The pair transformed Dundee into one of the fittest sides in the land and their close working relationship with the players helped generate a genuine family atmosphere at the club.

Anderson, Smith and Bennett were Dundee's 'Holy Trinity' and were as much Hampden Heroes as any of the players. They deserve their place amongst the greats of Dundee Football Club.

Reggie Smith

James Christopher Reginald Smith was born in Battersea, London on January 20th 1912. He was the son of a South African rugby internationalist, whose surname was actually Schmidt but it was the round rather than the oval ball that Reggie excelled in.

Reggie started his footballing career as an amateur with Hitchin Town in the early Thirties, playing in one of that club's finest teams and helped them to the Spartan League title in 1935. He turned professional when he joined Millwall later that year.

In 1936/37 he helped his new side to F.A. Cup semi-finals, the first time a team from the third tier of English football had reached that stage and in the next season Smith enjoyed even greater success as Millwall hurtled to the Division Three (South) title, while also claiming the London F.A. Challenge Cup by defeating Crystal Palace.

Reggie's form at The Den was rewarded with an England call-up and he became the last Millwall player to be capped by the 'Three Lions.' He was also the youngest player to play for England at the time when he scored twice on his debut in a 4-0 win over Norway at St James' Park on November 9th 1938 and followed that up a week later by starring in a 7-0 win over Northern Ireland at Old Trafford.

When the Second World War broke out in 1939, Smith, like many other footballers, found his career disrupted. He joined the R.A.F. and continued to appear sporadically for Millwall when his military schedule allowed. He was transferred to R.A.F. Leuchars in 1944 and subsequently turned out for Dundee as a guest in the war-time Scottish League North-East Division and was part of the side that won the First Series.

Originally an outside-left, he took up the left-half berth at Dens Park and when hostilities finished, he joined the Dark Blues on a permanent basis in March 1946, helping them win the 'B' Division titles in both 1945/46 and 1946/47. He made the most appearances of any player (35) in the 1947 promotion-winning campaign and he got on the scoresheet in the club record 10-0 win over Alloa on March 8th.

In Dundee's first year back in the top tier, Smith often assisted coaches Willie Cameron and Andy McCall with training and in 1948, he was appointed player-manager of Corby Town upon the club's formation. Just a few months later however he left Corby for family reasons and returned north to Dundee to become a coach.

When Willie Cameron retired eighteen months later, Smith was promoted to trainer-coach, effectively assistant manager, and would take charge of training on a daily basis. With Anderson coming down from his home in the Granite City just twice a week, Smith would handle any business in his absence and the players came to trust him as the first port of call.

On a matchday, Smith would be on the touchline with Anderson in the stand and he was in the dugout for the Dark Blues' three trips to the National Stadium in 1951 and 1952. Smith would take on a more crucial role when George Anderson became ill before the League Cup Final with Kilmarnock and was in charge on the big day at Hampden with Anderson resting at home. Reg would regularly travel up and down to Aberdeen to discuss club business with Anderson while he was recuperating and after defeating Kilmarnock 2-0 in the final, he took the trophy to the north-east as a surprise for his boss.

When Anderson resigned due to ill health two years later, Smith was surprisingly overlooked for the job and so instead he crossed the road to Tannadice to become manager of Dundee United. After two seasons of steady mid-table finishes, he resigned in January 1957 to take over as manager of Falkirk, then bottom of Division One and three months later, he had saved the 'Bairns' from relegation and led his new club to victory in the Scottish Cup.

In the summer of 1959, Smith took over as manager at his old club Millwall and later moved to South Africa to manage a number of clubs in the new National Football League. He returned to England in 1971 to manage Bedford Town and retired from the game in 1973.

Reggie sadly passed away in Stevenage on January 5th 2004, aged ninety-one but seven months before his death he was interviewed on the eve of Dundee's Scottish Cup Final with Rangers by the *Stevenage Comet* where he reminisced fondly about his own Hampden Cup Final with the men from Ibrox over five decades before.

Honours at Dundee:	
(As player)	
Scottish League 'B' Division winners:	1945/46, 1946/47
Scottish League North-East Division (First Series):	1944/45
(As coach)	
Scottish League Cup winners:	1951/52, 1952/53
Scottish League Championship runners-up:	1948/49
Scottish Cup runners-up:	1952
Appearances, Goals:	
League:	79, 10 goals
Scottish Cup:	4
League Cup:	9
Other:	4
Totals:	96, 10 goals

Reuben Bennett

Reuben Bennett was born in Aberdeen in December 1913 and started his football career as a goalkeeper with Aberdeen East End in 1930. It was while playing with an Aberdeen Junior Select against Hull City that Bennett impressed and he was offered terms and signed by the Boothferry Park side.

In 1936 he moved back north to Queen of the South after being released by Hull because of injury and he played for the Dumfries side until the outbreak of the Second World War.

After his war service Reuben signed for Dundee, having played for the club as a guest during the conflict and turned out for the Dark Blues ninety-four times in the next five years. Well known for his daring saves, the big keeper was part of the side to win the Scottish League North-East Division (First Series) in 1944/45. An excellent shot stopper who was also an expert at cutting out cross balls, he would then win two back to back 'B' Division title in 1946 and 1947 and in 1949, Bennett made four appearances as Dundee finished second in the Scottish League Championship.

By then he was at the veteran stage, sharing the goalkeeping duties with three other custodians and he hung his gloves up at the end of that runners-up season.

Almost immediately, Bennett was offered a coaching role at Dens and would work alongside Reggie Smith under manager George Anderson. Bennett proved himself to be an innovative coach alongside Smith and their newly devised training schedules had the Dundee players amongst the fittest in the land.

At the League Cup winners' reception after the 1951 final, skipper Alfie Boyd acknowledged the work of Bennett in his speech and at the end of the season chairman James Gellatly also thanked Bennett for his efforts in getting the players so fit.

For the Kilmarnock final twelve months later, Bennett was vital in assisting Smith during Anderson's absence and he was delighted when the Dark Blues won their second winners' medal in twelve months.

Just before the end of the season, Bennett moved to Ayr United to take up the manager's post, meaning he missed out on Dundee's trip to South Africa, but he discovered that management was not for him. He decided that coaching was his strength and in May 1955, he resigned to become assistant-trainer at Motherwell under Bobby Ancell, a former team mate at Dens.

He then became trainer at Third Lanark under Bob Shankly in 1959 but moved down south to Liverpool to take up a similar post at Anfield towards the end of manager Phil Taylor's reign. When Taylor resigned in November, his replacement was Bob's brother Bill Shankly and Shankly would go on to build Liverpool into his *"Bastion of invincibility."*

He created the infamous Anfield Boot Room, retaining the services of coaches Bob Paisley, Joe Fagan and Reuben Bennett. In this informal environment, between them they discussed tactics and plans, during which time Bennett was referred to as Sherlock, due to his preferred choice of headwear, a deerstalker. Thus the management philosophy behind Liverpool's success over the next three decades was born.

A fitness fanatic, at Liverpool Bennett was entrusted by Shankly with responsibility for player training and physical condition and indeed his whole outlook on the game was based on the premise that his players should be fitter than any other side and should be able to keep running longer than any other side; something he had preached successfully at Dens.

Reuben loved recounting his stories at Anfield, promoting the idea amongst the players that he was a hard man. He would tell tales about how he had played golf in Scotland on golf courses with bunkers so big, you needed a rope ladder to get in and out of them. He had a reputation for telling 'tall stories' - stories which many believed contained an element of truth but were embellished for the purposes of entertaining people. On one occasion he told Roy Evans that in a game for Dundee, he had gone in to challenge an oncoming striker and got concussion. He was carted off to hospital but decided he was fit enough to continue. Bennett insisted that he made his way back to the ground, paid at the turnstile to get back in the ground and then went back in goal and continued playing. Any other man telling this story would have been laughed at but even a wily Scouser like Evans wouldn't write off the possibility of this story being true - because he knew that Reuben Bennett was one of football's hard men.

Bennett was the only one of the original Anfield boot room quartet who didn't manage Liverpool and he stayed at the club until he retired.

He died aged seventy-six in December 1989 and although he is best remembered as a member of Bill Shankly's backroom team, he was a vital member of the Dark Blues coaching staff and one of Dundee's Hampden Heroes.

Honours at Dundee:

(As player)	
Scottish League 'B' Division winners:	1945/46, 1946/47
Scottish League North-East Division (First Series):	1944/45
Scottish League Championship runners-up:	1948/49
(As coach)	
Scottish League Cup winners:	1951/52, 1952/53
Scottish Cup runners-up:	1952
Appearances:	
League:	75
Scottish Cup:	3
League Cup:	10
Other:	6
Total:	94

George Anderson

"If you want to be big, think big," was Dundee managing/director's philosophy during his ten years in charge at Dens. He certainly practised what he preached when he brought the Dark Blues their first silverware in four decades, broke the world record transfer fee and brought Dundee within a whisker of being Champions of Scotland. His post-war time in charge was the most successful era in The Dark Blues' history and George Anderson deserves his place amongst the Dundee greats.

Anderson's first encounter with Dundee actually came as player during World War One when he was a guest from his parent club Aberdeen and played in goal in the 1917/18 season. At the end of the previous year Dundee had been asked to drop out of the Scottish League Division One until the end of the war to reduce travelling costs and so instead went into the Scottish League Eastern Division. Anderson was part of the successful Dark Blues side which won the league championship on goal average and won every cup competition they entered.

When he returned to Aberdeen at the end of the war, Anderson was awarded with a benefit match from The Dons and once again Dundee featured in his playing career when they provided the opposition.

By the start of the second global conflict in 1939, Anderson was a director at Pittodrie and was made team manager when the Dons manager Davie Halliday went off to war. Anderson enjoyed his caretaker position immensely but as it was being held open for Halliday's return, Anderson made a move for the position at Dens which had been left vacant when Dundee closed for the war in 1940.

Dundee returned in 1944 to play in the Scottish League North-East Division with Anderson in charge and joined the 'B' Division the following year having been relegated on the eve of war and he led his troops to both Championships in his first two years. In his third season, Dundee again won the 'B' Division to finally gain promotion to the top tier and Anderson became a hero in Dark Blue eyes.

Anderson was keen for a tilt at the top prize and after some shrewd recruitment led Dundee to the semi-finals of both the Scottish and League Cups and to runners-up in the 'A' Division in 1949 and was desperately unlucky not to win it.

In an effort to win some silverware however Anderson managed one of the greatest signings in the club's history when he splashed out a world record fee for Scottish superstar Billy Steel, having fought off stiff competition from Rangers for his signature. The fee was £23,500; extraordinary for a provincial club like Dundee to pay such an incredible fee and Anderson's philosophy of *'think big'* was repaid when silverware was soon on its way to Dens.

Anderson, who liked to watch the game from the directors' box, led Dundee to their first ever League Cup win over Rangers in October 1951 and repeated that feat twelve months later with victory over Kilmarnock at Hampden. In between times Dundee appeared in the Scottish Cup Final and Anderson had finally turned Dundee into a trophy-winning, Scottish football force.

He missed the final against Killie having been taken ill with pleurisy shortly before and just two years later had to resign his post of manager due to ill health, retaining his seat on the board and left as Dundee's oldest serving manager at the age of sixty-seven.

His departure marked the end of the Dark Blues' post-war golden age but Anderson had done much to lay the foundations of Dundee Football Club as a prominent force in Scottish football. He has won more trophies than any other manager since Dundee's formation and he saw his dream of a successful club come true. In 2003 he was listed in the top fifty Scottish managers of all time by *The Sunday Herald* and raised the profile and the stature of Dundee Football Club. Anderson's legacy was set and the foundations were in place for the Dark Blues to move to the next level within the next decade.

It's appropriate that the last word is about George Anderson as he was the leader and the pioneer of Dundee's Hampden Heroes and that group of men rightly have a special place in the wonderful history of Dundee Football Club.

Honours at Dundee:	
(As player)	
Scottish League Eastern Division winners:	1917/18
Penman Cup winners:	1917/18
Loftus Cup winners:	1917/18
Eastern Cup winners (joint with Dundee Hibernian):	1917/18
(As manager)	
Scottish League Cup winners:	1951/52, 1952/53
Scottish League Championship runners-up:	1948/49
Scottish Cup runners-up:	1952
Scottish League 'B' Division winners:	1945/46, 1946/47
Scottish League North-East Division (first series):	1944/45

Appearances:	
League:	17
Penman Cup:	3
Loftus Cup:	3
Eastern Cup:	1
Total:	24

Managerial Record with Dundee (1944–1954)

	P	W	D	L	F	A	Pts
League:	298	161	53	84	684	435	379
Scottish Cup:	26	13	5	8	55	36	
League Cup:	63	34	10	19	140	97	
Other:	10	5	2	3	20	17	
Total:	397	213	70	114	834	585	

Chapter 35:
The Roads to Hampden

THE FOLLOWING IS a summary of the matches en route to the three cup finals in 1951 and 1952:

1951/52 Scottish League Cup:

Date	Opponents	Round	Score	Scorers	Crowd
Aug 11th	St. Mirren (a)	Section C	2-2	Toner, Flavell	12,000

Line-up: Henderson, Follon, Frew, Gallacher, Boyd, Cowie, Flavell, Toner, Ziesing, Steel, Andrews

Aug 15th	Heart of Midlothian (h)	Section C	2-1	Ziesing (2)	22,500

Line up: Henderson, Follon, Cowan, Gallacher, Cowie, Boyd, Flavell, Toner, Ziesing, Steel, Andrews

Aug 18th	Raith Rovers (h)	Section C	5-0	Steel, Toner (3), Colville (o.g.)	21,000

Line-up: Henderson, Follon, Frew, Gallacher, Cowie, Boyd, Flavell, Toner, Ziesing, Steel, Andrews

Aug 25th	St. Mirren (h)	Section C	0-1		21,000

Line-up: Bobby Henderson, Follon, Frew, Gallacher, Bert Henderson, Boyd, Flavell, Toner, Ziesing, Steel, Andrews

Aug 29th	Heart of Midlothian (a)	Section C	2-5	Toner, Ziesing	30,000

Line-up: Henderson, Follon, Frew, Gallacher, Cowie, Boyd, Flavell, Toner, Ziesing, Steel, Christie

Sep 1st	Raith Rovers (a)	Section C	3-1	Christie (2), Williams	12,400

Line-up: Brown, Follon, Frew, Irvine, Cowie, Boyd, Ewen, Toner, Ziesing, Williams, Christie

Sep 15th	Falkirk (a)	Quarter-final 1st leg	0-0		12,000

Line-up: Brown, Follon, Frew, Irvine, Cowie, Boyd, Flavell, Toner, Copland, Williams, Christie

Sep 20th	Falkirk (h)	Quarter-final 2nd leg	2-1 (2-1 agg)	Ziesing, Steel	20,000

Line-up: Brown, Follon, Frew, Irvine, Cowie, Boyd, Hill, Williams, Ziesing, Steel, Christie

Oct 13th	Motherwell (Ibrox)	Semi-final	5-1	Christie, Flavell (3), Pattillo	31,000

Line-up: Brown, Follon, Cowan, Gallacher, Cowie, Boyd, Toner, Pattillo, Flavell, Steel, Christie

Oct 27th	Rangers (Hampden)	Final	3-2	Flavell, Pattillo, Boyd	92,325

Line-up: Brown, Follon, Cowan, Gallacher, Cowie, Boyd, Toner, Pattillo, Flavell, Steel, Christie

For the Record:
Scottish League Cup – 'A' Division, Section C

Team	Pld	W	D	L	GF	GA	GAv	Pts
Dundee	6	3	1	2	14	10	1.40	7
Heart of Midlothian	6	3	1	2	15	12	1.25	7
St. Mirren	6	2	2	2	13	13	1.00	6
Raith Rovers	6	2	0	4	6	13	0.46	4

Appearances, Goals:

Alfie Boyd:	10 appearances, 1 goal
Gerry Follon:	10 appearances
Jimmy Toner:	9 appearances, 5 goals
Doug Cowie:	9 appearances
Bobby Flavell:	8 appearances, 5 goals
Billy Steel:	8 appearances, 2 goals
Ken Ziesing:	7 appearances, 4 goals
Gordon Frew:	7 appearances
Tommy Gallacher:	7 appearances
George Christie:	6 appearances, 3 goals
Bill Brown:	5 appearances
Bobby Henderson:	5 appearances
Stan Williams:	3 appearances, 1 goal
Jack Cowan:	3 appearances
Andy Irvine:	3 appearances
Johnny Pattillo:	2 appearances, 2 goals
Ernie Copland:	1 appearance
Ernie Ewen:	1 appearance
Bob Henderson:	1 appearance
George Hill:	1 appearance

Number of Players Used	-	20
Matches Played	-	10
Number of Wins	-	6
Number of Draws	-	2
Number of Defeats	-	2
Number of Goals Scored	-	24
Number of Goals Conceded	-	14
Top Goal Scorer	-	Bobby Flavell & Jimmy Toner (5 goals each)
Highest Home Attendance	-	22,500 v Hearts, Sectional Tie, 15/8/1951
Highest Away Attendance	-	30,000 v Hearts, Sectional Tie, 29/8/1951
Highest Neutral Attendance	-	92,325 v Rangers, Final, 27/10/1951
Total Attendance	-	274,225
Average Attendance	-	27,423
Highest Win	-	5-1 v Motherwell, Semi-Final, 13/10/1951
Biggest Defeat	-	2-5 v Hearts, Sectional Tie, 29/8/1951
Clean Sheets	-	2
Failed to Score:	-	2

1951/52 Scottish Cup:

Date	Opponents	Round	Score	Scorers	Crowd
Jan 26th	Ayr United (h)	1st Round	4-0	Irvine (2), Pattillo, Steel	20,000

Line-up: Henderson, Follon, Cowan, Gallacher, Cowie, Boyd, Hill, Pattillo, Irvine, Steel, Christie

Date	Opponents	Round	Score	Scorers	Crowd
Feb 9th	Wigtown & Bladnoch (a)	2nd Round	7-1	Steel (2), Pattillo (2), Hill (2), Christie	4,500

Line-up: Henderson, Follon, Cowan, Gallacher, Cowie, Boyd, Hill, Pattillo, Irvine, Steel, Christie

Date	Opponents	Round	Score	Scorers	Crowd
Feb 23rd	Berwick Rangers (h)	3rd Round	1-0	Pattillo	15,000

Line-up: Henderson, Follon, Cowan, Gallacher, Cowie, Boyd, Hill, Pattillo, Flavell, Steel, Christie

Date	Opponents	Round	Score	Scorers	Crowd
Mar 8th	Aberdeen (h)	Quarter-final	4-0	Ziesing, Steel (2), Boyd (pen)	41,000

Line-up: Henderson, Follon, Cowan, Gallacher, Cowie, Boyd, Burrell, Pattillo, Ziesing, Steel, Christie

Date	Opponents	Round	Score	Scorers	Crowd
Mar 29th	Third Lanark (Easter Road)	Semi-Final	2-0	Burrell, Steel	23,615

Line-up: Henderson, Follon, Cowan, Gallacher, Cowie, Boyd, Burrell, Pattillo, Flavell, Steel, Christie

Date	Opponents	Round	Score	Scorers	Crowd
Apr 19th	Motherwell (Hampden)	Final	0-4		136,990

Line-up: Henderson, Follon, Cowan, Gallacher, Cowie, Boyd, Hill, Pattillo, Flavell, Steel, Christie

For the Record:
Appearances, Goals:

Billy Steel:	6 appearances, 6 goals
Johnny Pattillo:	6 appearances, 4 goals
Alfie Boyd:	6 appearances, 1 goal
George Christie:	6 appearances, 1 goal
Gerry Follon:	6 appearances
Doug Cowie:	6 appearances
Tommy Gallacher:	6 appearances
Jack Cowan:	6 appearances
Bobby Henderson:	6 appearances
George Hill:	4 appearances, 2 goals
Bobby Flavell:	3 appearances
Andy Irvine:	2 appearances, 2 goals
Gerry Burrell:	2 appearances, 1 goal
Ken Ziesing:	1 appearance, 1 goal

Number of Players Used	-	14
Matches Played	-	6
Number of Wins	-	5
Number of Draws	-	0
Number of Defeats	-	1
Number of Goals Scored	-	18
Number of Goals Conceded	-	5

Top Goal Scorer	-	Billy Steel (6 goals)
Highest Home Attendance	-	41,000 v Aberdeen, Quarter-final, 8/3/1952
Highest Away Attendance	-	4,500 v Wigtown & Bladnoch, 2nd Round, 9/2/1952
Highest Neutral Attendance	-	136,990 v Motherwell, Final, 19/4/1952
Total Attendance	-	241,105
Average Attendance	-	40,184
Highest Win	-	7-1 v Wigtown & Bladnoch, 2nd Round, 9/2/1952
Biggest Defeat	-	0-4 v Motherwell, Final, 19/4/1952
Clean Sheets	-	4
Failed to Score:	-	1

1952/53 Scottish League Cup:

Date	Opponents	Round	Score	Scorers	Crowd
Aug 9th	Raith Rovers (h)	Section D	2-1	Burrell, Christie	20,000

Line-up: Henderson, Frew, Cowan, Ziesing, Boyd, Cowie, Burrell, Toner, Flavell, Steel, Christie

Aug 13th	Airdrieonians (a)	Section D	3-1	Flavell (3)	12,000

Line-up: Henderson, Frew, Cowan, Ziesing, Merchant, Cowie, Burrell, Toner, Flavell, Steel, Christie

Aug 16th	Clyde (h)	Section D	2-2	Flavell, Steel	21,000

Line-up: Henderson, Frew, Cowan, Ziesing, Merchant, Cowie, Burrell, Toner, Flavell, Steel, Christie,

Aug 23rd	Raith Rovers (a)	Section D	2-1	Steel (2)	17,000

Line-up: Henderson, Follon, Cowan, Ziesing, Boyd, Cowie, Burrell, Gallacher, Flavell, Steel, Christie

Aug 27th	Airdrieonians (h)	Section D	3-2	Flavell (2), Toner	19,000

Line-up: Henderson, Follon, Cowan, Ziesing, Boyd, Cowie, Toner, Gallacher, Flavell, Steel, Christie

Aug 30th	Clyde (a)	Section D	3-3	Christie, Boyd (pen), Toner	18,000

Line-up: Henderson, Follon, Cowan, Ziesing, Boyd, Cowie, Toner, Gallacher, Flavell, Steel, Christie

Sep 13th	Stirling Albion (a)	Quarter-final 1st leg,	1-3	Burrell	8,000

Line-up: B. Henderson, Follon, Cowan, Gallacher, Boyd, Ziesing, Burrell, A. Henderson, Flavell, Steel, Christie

Sep 17th	Stirling Albion (h)	Quarter-final 2nd leg	5-0 (6-3 agg.)	Flavell (2), Steel (2), Boyd (pen)	24,000

Line-up: b. Henderson, Follon, Cowan, Ziesing, Boyd, Cowie, Toner, A. Henderson, Flavell, Steel, Christie

Oct 4th	Hibernian (Tynecastle)	Semi-final	2-1	Steel, Flavell	44,200

Line-up: B. Henderson, Follon, Cowan, Ziesing, Boyd, Cowie, Toner, A. Henderson, Flavell, Steel, Christie

Oct 25th	Kilmarnock (Hampden)	Final	2-0	Flavell (2)	51,000

Line-up: B. Henderson, Follon, Frew, Ziesing, Boyd, Cowie, Roner, A. Henderson, Flavell, Steel, Christie

For the Record:

Scottish League Cup – 'A' Division, Section D

Team	Pld	W	D	L	GF	GA	GAv	Pts
Dundee	6	4	2	0	15	10	1.50	10
Clyde	6	1	3	2	15	15	1.00	5
Raith Rovers	6	2	1	3	9	14	0.64	5
Airdrieonians	6	1	2	3	9	9	1.00	4

Appearances, Goals:

Bobby Flavell:	10 appearances, 11 goals
Billy Steel:	10 appearances, 6 goals
George Christie:	10 appearances, 2 goals
Ken Ziesing:	10 appearances
Bobby Henderson:	10 appearances
Doug Cowie:	9 appearances
Jack Cowan:	9 appearances
Alfie Boyd:	8 appearances, 2 goals
Jimmy Toner:	8 appearances, 2 goals
Gerry Follon:	7 appearances
Gerry Burrell:	5 appearances, 2 goals
Tommy Gallacher:	4 appearances
Albert Henderson:	4 appearances
Gordon Frew:	4 appearances
George Merchant:	2 appearances

Number of Players Used	-	15
Matches Played	-	10
Number of Wins	-	7
Number of Draws	-	2
Number of Defeats	-	1
Number of Goals Scored	-	25
Number of Goals Conceded	-	14
Top Goal Scorer	-	Bobby Flavell (11 goals)
Highest Home Attendance	-	24,000 v Stirling Albion, Quarter-final 2nd leg, 17/9/1952
Highest Away Attendance	-	18,000 v Clyde, Sectional Tie, 30/8/1952
Highest Neutral Attendance	-	51,000 v Kilmarnock, Final, 25/10/1952
Total Attendance	-	234,200
Average Attendance	-	23,420
Highest Win	-	5-0 v Stirling Albion, Quarter-final 2nd leg, 17/9/1952
Biggest Defeat	-	1-3 v Stirling Albion, Quarter-final 1st leg, 13/9/1952
Clean Sheets	-	2
Failed to Score:	-	0